The
Fabulous
Baker
Brothers
Glorious British Grub

Glorious British Grub

Henry & Tom Herbert

headline

To Trevor and Polly Herbert

First published in 2013
by HEADLINE PUBLISHING GROUP

1

Cataloguing in Publication Data is available from the British Library

978 0 7553 64619

Project Editor: Mari Roberts
Designed by Smith & Gilmour, London
Food Styling: Richard Harris
Recipe Tester: Signe Johansen
Fabulous Baker Brothers logo by Brad Evans

Printed and bound in Great Britain by Butler Tanner & Dennis

Headline's policy is to use papers that are natural, renewable and recyclable products and
made from wood grown in sustainable forests. The logging and manufacturing processes
are expected to conform to the environmental regulations of the country of origin.

HEADLINE PUBLISHING GROUP
An Hachette UK Company
338 Euston Road
London NW1 3BH

www.headline.co.uk
www.hachette.co.uk

This book is published to accompany the television series *The Fabulous Baker Brothers* produced by Betty TV.

CONTENTS

There's a great feeling of pride about British food at the moment. Wherever people are from, they are proud of the food that's being produced in their area, and they are celebrating it. That became very clear to us over the past year as we travelled around the country, giving demos, doing tastings and samplings at festivals, taking part in discussions and meeting great food producers. Barely a weekend has gone by that we haven't been in some part of the United Kingdom sampling wonderful local produce and meeting inspiring people. It has been really exciting. But we also saw that there are places where, as a nation, we seem to be missing the mark. There's great food around, but you have to have a nose for it. If you're a visitor, you might well be missing out altogether.

So we've also been on the road this year making a new TV series, cooking dishes in popular sightseeing destinations. We visited six towns and cities, all tourist hotspots: London, Stratford, York, Blackpool, Exmouth, and, close to home for us, Bourton-on-the-Water in the Cotswolds.

Tom: 'You get millions of visitors to Britain every year. One of the main reasons they come here is for our wealth of history and heritage. Yet one of their main disappointments is the food. We wanted to show the tourists, along with the locals, that this needn't be the case.'

Henry: 'People go to the Tower of London, and they come out saying, "Wow, we saw the Crown Jewels, it's amazing – now let's get something to eat," but what's on offer and easy to get is often not the best. Perhaps they only have to go a few streets back to find somewhere better, but tourists generally don't do that, because they don't have time, or the guidebook doesn't tell them, or they've got to get back on their bus. So they end up with this great experience of the buildings, and this bad experience of the food. We want to change that.'

Tom: 'The number-one thing tourists eat is fish and chips, even if they are in Stratford, or Bourton-on the-Water, which are landlocked. So we rock up in our van – it's a Morris Minor, really pretty – in one of these places and we've got stuff in the back, we've got camping gas, and we get out the trestle tables and start cooking. First of all we do a trial dish, to see what the local ingredients are, what we can do with them and how people react to it. In London, it was crayfish; we put garlic and chilli in a frying pan, added some oil, got it really hot, put the crayfish in, then, just as they were glazing, we poured in some Sipsmith gin and flambéed it. We added lemon zest and paprika to crème fraîche and mixed it in with the crayfish, and served it in leaves of Little Gem—'

Henry: 'And meanwhile a crowd has gathered—'

Tom: 'And so we hand them out to fifty, a hundred people, and say, this is made with Thames crayfish and London gin – do you like it? And they say yes. And then we ask them what kind of food they've been eating, and they say fish and chips. Did you like that? Not so much.'

The trial dish was our way of introducing ourselves. We also worked with a local establishment, one that was much visited by tourists but perhaps had lost its way a bit. We never wanted to be nasty, but we did want to be honest, so we would ask whether they felt the people who visited their restaurant really did enjoy the food. (Because more often than not, *we* didn't!) Then we'd come up with three dishes we felt suited the establishment, and also represented the town or city we were in. And that would be different in sugar-charged, lit-up Blackpool, where the energy is ramped right up, to calm and gentle Bourton-on-the-Water. We wanted the dishes to represent the place we were in – to tell the visitors something about where they were, and also to remind the locals of the great produce they had – but we wanted to do it in a realistic, achievable way.

Take Exmouth. You could see where the mackerel was, you could watch the beef cattle on the surrounding hillsides, you could find a mussel farm – and yet a lot of the visitors were eating frozen scampi. For us it wasn't just about going to the local organic farmer, it was also about finding the heartbeat of the town, the pace of the town. You meet the people; find out who lives there, what they eat and what they do. In Exmouth we met shanty singers, great characters, and thanks to their singing songs about the local tradition of smuggling spirits, we ended up with brandy in our recipes.

Henry: 'It was about coming up with dishes that were right for the place.'

Tom: 'Like the Blackpool Pleasure Cake [see page 127], a big cake with smashed rock and popping candy in it, and candy floss on top. And LED lights around it. And kiss-me-quick lips.'

In Blackpool, hot doughnuts are sold everywhere. There also used to be a big tradition of Morecambe Bay shrimps, but this has almost died out. So we created doughnuts called Fiery Fish Balls (see page 238). We made really strong anchovy aioli and folded the shrimps through, then wrapped it in a doughnut and deep-fried it. Afterwards the doughnuts were rolled in salt, sugar, paprika and cayenne.

Henry: 'They are strong, dirty and deep-fried and they blow your mind, but people love them. It's kind of what Blackpool is. It's not subdued, it's in your face. And for us it's like, let's make a doughnut to help fuel this.'

In each place, we'd get the café or restaurant on side. They would make the three dishes we'd come up with, and we'd all put them to the public vote.

Henry: 'The meat pie always wins!'

Tom: 'Not in Blackpool. They loved the Pleasure Cake.'

Some of the businesses were coping with the reality of having masses of people coming to their inappropriately small place. Or they had to be fiercely competitive with other businesses, and ended up in a downward spiral. Or they gave up in the face of crowds of tourists who didn't have high expectations and whom they would never see again.

One lady we were working with had once won a scone-making competition. Some years later she and her partner took over a tea shop in the Cotswolds. It was the fulfilment of a dream and they had so many ideas about what they wanted to do, but it was incredibly busy and they were struggling. The first person to offer help was an ingredients supplier who sold them a scone premix, and that was that.

Tom: 'I once spent two weeks in Japan making scones by hand to encourage Japanese people to come to the Cotswolds, and the first thing they eat when they do come is a premix that they complain tastes of chewing-gum! So we had a scone-off, me and Sue, the tea shop lady. My scones actually took less time than her premix ones, and they tasted way better. I was able to show her that she could make her own scones and freeze them, and get one of her afternoon kids to bake off a couple of dozen as required. She hadn't thought how to use her own award-winning scone recipe like this. I hope we got her back on track. And that's how it becomes a compassionate story. I think some of the people we met were a bit stuck and we were thrilled that we could help them re-engage with that dream they had about doing good food.'

We've had an incredible year. As well as the travelling, and the new TV series, we were part of the London Olympics. We created a range of barbecue recipes for people to cook at home on Super Saturday. Food for people who couldn't get to the games but wanted to feel involved on that amazing day. We also worked with catering company Create for the Paralympics launch party at Old Billingsgate, with 800 guests. We've been to Number 10 as part of a celebration of the best British food, organized by Visit Britain and the Sustainable Restaurant Association. Getting Chris Evans into bread again, live on his breakfast show, was quite a moment. And back at home, Hobbs House Bakery won Apprentice of the Year once again, so we are training the new generation.

Henry: 'Tom was the *Cotswold Life* Food Hero of the Year.'

Tom: 'Which was overwhelming, and a total surprise.'

Family members and colleagues stepped into our work roles at home while we were away. Ours is still a small company – you could say that in our ninety years of being in business, we've spectacularly grown really small! Our ethics are about sourcing locally, being fiercely independent, being creative and having an impact in the community.

After the travelling, it was wonderful to be back at home, cooking for family and friends. Not banquets, just great home cooking. We've included all the pie recipes from our first series in this book, as well as all the recipes from this, our second series, plus our favourite dishes from home. Some of these dishes are classics, updated for today, while others are new British dishes that have become part of our repertoire as we have been influenced and inspired by other cultures and cuisines.

All this gallivanting has been great fun, but there's nothing quite like that feeling of knowing you are going home. Sometimes you need soul food, you need home-cooking. If life is hectic, at home is where you readjust and get back to something that's good and honest and true. And if you take food that's good and homely and comforting, but make it with amazing produce, then it goes from being good home food to glorious home food. And that's really what this book is all about.

Tom and Henry

www.hobbshousebakery.co.uk

BREAK
OF DAY

TOM

Day break is the baker's breakfast time, between
4 a.m. and 7.30 a.m. It's also when you might be
getting up early to go on holiday. No one should
ever eat between 2 a.m. and 4 a.m. – that ought
to be a law. I've done all the shifts and you just
can't eat between those two hours!

HENRY

Any of these makes a very good start to
the day, whatever time you have to get up.
The bacon butty does it for me.

OVERNIGHT PORRIDGE

HIGHLAND PORRIDGE

FIRE PORRIDGE

OAT CRUNCH

BACON BUTTY

BACON PORRIDGE

HOME-MADE KETCHUP

HOME-CURED BACON

FIERY GINGER NUTS

TEA-SOAKED DRIED FRUIT

OVERNIGHT PORRIDGE

··· SERVES 2 ···

Tom: This is the most hair-shirt hard-core breakfast I know and will blow a stiff breeze up your kilt any cold morning. A bowl of this will power even the most ferocious haggis hunter until lunchtime. Pinhead oatmeal needs a bit more effort than rolled oats to make into porridge but it's worth it for the lovely, chewy texture. Pinhead oatmeal absorbs water very slowly, whether the water is hot or cold, so the best thing is to soak it overnight. If you make a cup of mint tea or cocoa before bed, then that's the time to put this in the pan ready for the morning. Serve with milk and honey, or what you fancy.

| 1 cup pinhead or coarse oatmeal | 2 cups water | pinch of salt |

1 Put the ingredients in a pan with the lid on and leave overnight to soften.

2 In the morning, put the pan on a medium heat and stir until thickened and porridgey: about 3 minutes. Turn the heat off, put the lid back on (or porridge bowls, to warm them) and leave for 5 minutes before eating.

3 If you have an Aga-type oven, you can leave the pan in the coolest part overnight, such as in the plate-warming oven, and it will not only be softened and thickened by the morning but it should be warm enough to eat straight away. It's the same if you have a wood-burning stove that retains heat overnight.

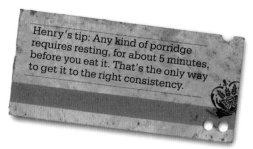

Henry's tip: Any kind of porridge requires resting, for about 5 minutes, before you eat it. That's the only way to get it to the right consistency.

HIGHLAND PORRIDGE

··· SERVES 2 ···

Tom: Lost in the highlands, snow falling all around, Anna heavy with child and with nowhere to stay the night, we felt like a modern, northern version of Mary and Joseph. At last we happened on a hunting lodge, not yet open for the season. The laird took pity on our predicament and welcomed us in. We slept in warm beds with the wind and snow thrashing at the window and the promise of the best porridge ever in the morning.

A log fire in the breakfast room warmed the place and the windows on three sides revealed a panoramic Highland winter scene. 'Your oats are from the hillock there,' pointed out the owner. 'Your cream is out the wee golden Highland cattle here. 'Tis sweetened with a spoon of fine heather honey, and, to light a fire in your belly, a wee tot of my very own single malt whisky.' This without doubt is the most welcome breakfast I've ever eaten. Starting the day the laird way.

| 1 cup porridge oats | 1 cup full-fat milk | cream, honey and whisky, to serve |
| 1 cup water | pinch of sea salt | |

1 Put the oats, water, milk and salt in a pan and stir over a medium heat until slightly thickened: about 3–5 minutes. Then put the lid on (or your porridge bowls, to warm them) and rest it for 5 minutes.

2 Put in the bowl, dollop some double cream and honey on top, to taste. Serve with a shot of whisky, to be stirred in at the table.

FIRE PORRIDGE
··· SERVES 4 ···

Tom: My kids developed an expensive taste for strawberry cereal, to the point where we were getting through a pack a day. I had to create something to trump it, and this is it. I give you . . . FIRE porridge. This is now the go-to breakfast in the Herbert house. The kids dig it, it's way cheaper than shop-bought cereal, and it's got to be good for us. A win-win-win situation. A blowtorch adds the right degree of culinary theatre, but if you don't have one, use an overhead grill.

2 cups porridge oats

4 cups cold fresh milk, plus extra to serve

Demerara sugar, to serve

1 If you haven't got a kitchen blowtorch, preheat an overhead grill to hot.

2 Put the oats and milk into a saucepan and stir over a medium heat until the porridge has thickened into a dollopy, porridgey consistency: about 3–5 minutes. Turn the heat off, put the saucepan lid on and leave for 5 minutes until it is of the right consistency.

3 Portion into heatproof breakfast bowls (not plastic). Sprinkle a spoonful of Demerara sugar over each one, and blast with a blowtorch or under the grill until melted and blistered. Serve with a jug of cold milk to pour into a moat around the burnished porridge.

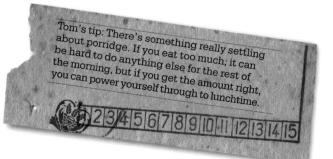

Tom's tip: There's something really settling about porridge. If you eat too much, it can be hard to do anything else for the rest of the morning, but if you get the amount right, you can power yourself through to lunchtime.

OAT CRUNCH

··· MAKES ABOUT 500G ···

A nice bit of easy, delicious, healthy baking – great to do opportunistically when you have a warm oven. You can fine-tune the taste to personal preference. Buy the ingredients in bulk to make it cheaper. Splash some cold milk over a bowl of this in the morning and you're good to go. Kids love it too. It's another great alternative to packets of breakfast cereal. You can also use it as a topping on baked fruit for pudding – with the leftovers for breakfast – or mix it with fresh fruit, honey and yogurt into a big bowl when you've got lots of overnight guests at the breakfast table.

300g porridge or jumbo oats	45g pumpkin seeds	120ml pure maple syrup (or honey)
75g flaked almonds	¼ tsp salt	
45g sunflower seeds	2 tbsp veg oil	

1 Heat the oven to 150°C/Gas 2. Line a baking tray with baking paper. Mix all the ingredients in a bowl until well coated, then spread over the lined tray in a layer about 1cm thick.

2 Bake in the oven for up to an hour, giving it a good stir after 30 minutes. Keep an eye on it: the darker it is, the crunchier it will be, but be warned it can quickly turn from brown to burned.

3 Remove from the oven and allow to cool. It keeps in a sealed tub for a month, easy.

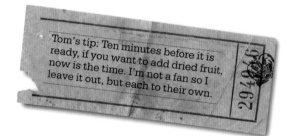

Tom's tip: Ten minutes before it is ready, if you want to add dried fruit, now is the time. I'm not a fan so I leave it out, but each to their own.

BACON BUTTY

⋯ SERVES 2 ⋯

Tom: This is something Henry and I have when we've got an early start. If I'm driving, the deal is that Henry makes the bacon butty. Then we set off and leave the butty as long as possible, with its smell filling up the van, until we can't resist it any longer. This really is a simple recipe: bacon and ketchup in a floury bap. But you can cure the bacon, make the ketchup and bake the bap (see page 46), and turn it into a monstrous undertaking . . .

Henry: Nothing quells the pangs of morning hunger like a bacon butty. The joy of a soft bap with lashings of tomato ketchup and a pile of crispy salty bacon encased in rich butter – nothing quite 'chews the fat' like proper bacon. To have made all the elements personally is to take the bacon butty to the next level. What early breakfast could be better?

| home-cured bacon (page 22) | 4 thick slices good white bread | home-made ketchup (facing page) |
| butter | or 2 soft baps (page 46) | |

1 The easy bit. Fry slices of your home-cure in a frying pan, butter the bread or baps and lather with ketchup. Absolutely perfect.

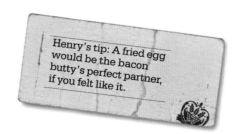

Henry's tip: A fried egg would be the bacon butty's perfect partner, if you felt like it.

HOME-MADE KETCHUP

··· MAKES 2 X 500G JARS ···

Who doesn't love ketchup? And yet, until you've made your own, you'll never know how good ketchup can really be. This is so worth the small effort it takes. If you sterilize and seal the jars, you can keep them on the shelf for months. Once opened, of course, you'll need to consume the ketchup in a week, but that shouldn't be difficult.

5 tbsp olive oil	1 short cinnamon stick	3 tbsp tomato purée
4 onions, very roughly chopped	1 tsp allspice berries	½ tsp Tabasco sauce
2 sticks of celery, very roughly chopped	½ tsp ground black pepper	150ml white wine vinegar
4 garlic cloves, sliced	2 tsp celery salt or salt	150g caster sugar
1 tsp ground coriander	2kg ripe tomatoes, roughly chopped	

1 In a saucepan, heat the olive oil and add the onion, celery and garlic. Sweat on a gentle heat for 5 minutes until soft. Add the spices and the tomatoes. Bring to a bubble and add the purée, Tabasco, vinegar and sugar. Turn the heat down low and cook for 1 hour or until the liquid has reduced down and the tomatoes are all soft.

2 Using a stick blender, whizz it up, then pass it through a sieve. Taste and tweak the seasoning. The ketchup may feel a little runny but it will thicken as it cools. Keep in the fridge for immediate use, or in a sterilized jar on a shelf for longer-term usage.

3 To sterilize jars for the ketchup (or any other preserving purpose), place the empty jars and their lids in the oven at 180°C/Gas 4 for 5 minutes. Remove, fill with ketchup, taking care not to spill any ketchup over the edges, and put the lids on. Place the jar or jars in a pan filled with boiling water to just below the level of the jar lids and boil for 10 minutes. This creates a vacuum in the jar, and the ketchup will keep for months until opened, during which time the flavour continues to develop. After opening, it will keep for a week. If you don't preserve it in this way, the ketchup will still keep for a week in a clean jar in the fridge.

HOME-CURED BACON

··· MAKES ABOUT 750G BACON ···

Henry: Curing is neither difficult nor lengthy. There is a perception that curing meats takes years, even generations of experience and many months of waiting. This may apply to a prime serrano ham, but simple curing like bacon is easy and can be done within a week. When I started at the butcher's I took up curing with great enthusiasm. I read every book and scoured the internet for tips and tricks, but all I was left with was a confused and sore head and little appetite to make my own. Thankfully I got over this and found that it is really quite simple.

1kg piece of boneless, rindless pork loin, ideally with a good layer of fat	**FOR THE CURE:** 400g fine sea salt 200g brown sugar 20g saltpetre, optional (from your local butcher's)	20g peppercorns few sprigs of thyme 4 bay leaves 1 tsp juniper berries 1 tsp coriander seeds

1 Mix the cure ingredients together in a bowl. The saltpetre is optional but will give your bacon a pleasant pink colour when cooked.

2 Scatter a third of the mix on the bottom of a dish that's large enough for your piece of pork. Place the pork loin, fat-side down, in the cure. Now massage the remaining cure over the rest of the pork. There should be a thin layer over the whole piece. Place a plate or board on top and weigh it down with a few tins. This will help to squeeze the water out of the pork as the cure penetrates the meat. Place in a cold fridge for 7 days. This is ample time for the pork to become bacon.

3 Remove from the fridge, wash the cure off the bacon and dab dry with a clean cloth. The bacon is ready, but it is better if left in the fridge for a day to firm up. Keeps in the fridge for 2 weeks.

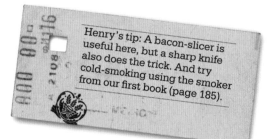

Henry's tip: A bacon-slicer is useful here, but a sharp knife also does the trick. And try cold-smoking using the smoker from our first book (page 185).

BACON PORRIDGE
··· SERVES 6 ···

Tom: This is a dish that was always made by our grandpa John Wells, who lived in a hamlet called Marefield in Leicestershire. When we used to stay there as kids, it was the highlight of our visit. Typically we'd arrive late and be bundled into bed, and in the morning the house would be full of the most incredible smell of cooking bacon as Grandpa would make, without fail, 'Marefield pie'. (Grandpa called all dishes he liked 'pies', and this was his star dish.) Eating it is a kind of initiation rite for newcomers to the family: you're one of us once you've had Marefield pie in pyjamas in the morning. It uses pinhead oatmeal, which is hard, and slowly absorbs the juices from tomatoes and bacon. You need old-school curly parsley, which has a stronger flavour than flat-leaf. Then you serve it on thick, hot buttered toast, ideally overnight dough (like the Hobbs House Sherston) or sourdough, and put a poached egg on top. Bit of mustard on the side and you're done. It's also good cold if there's any left over, but there rarely is. This is something we have at the beginning of every good day: at Christmastime, at Easter, at weddings . . . It's such a lush aroma that it gets everybody out of bed in the morning.

2 tbsp olive oil	5 tbsp chopped curly parsley	6 slices bread, toasted and thickly buttered
12 rashers smoked streaky bacon	1 tbsp white wine vinegar	
3 x 400g tins chopped tomatoes	6 free-range eggs	
150g pinhead or coarse oatmeal		

1 Heat the olive oil in a large sauté pan over a medium heat, then add the bacon and cook until it is just crispy and has released its fat. Pour in the tomatoes, mix well and bring to a simmer, then add the oatmeal and cook for 1 minute. Add the parsley, mix well, then cover, turn the heat off and leave for 10–15 minutes. The oatmeal will swell and cook in the heat of the mixture; it should be like a thick risotto.

2 Bring a pan of water to the boil, add the vinegar and crack in the eggs, 2 at a time, and poach for 2–3 minutes until done to your liking. Remove and dunk into iced water until ready to serve. (This takes the pressure off the cook when making poached eggs for a lot of people.) Drop back into simmering water for 30 seconds to heat through, then drain on kitchen paper.

3 Serve the bacon porridge on the toasted and buttered bread with a poached egg on top.

FIERY GINGER NUTS

··· MAKES 16 ···

These are perfect with a cup of tea (or coffee), and great dunkers. Packet ginger biscuits just don't compare to this. If you like ginger biscuits, you are going to love these. Surprisingly good first thing in the morning, when the ginger surprises your system into action.

75g unsalted butter	2 tsp baking powder	3 tsp ground ginger
2 tbsp caster sugar	½ tsp bicarbonate of soda	1½ tbsp Golden Syrup
75g wholemeal flour	1½ tsp cinnamon	45g chopped stem ginger

1 Heat the oven to 200°C/Gas 6. Line a large baking tray with baking parchment (or 2 smaller trays if you don't have a large one).

2 Cream the butter and sugar, by hand or with an electric beater. Then sift all the dry ingredients over the creamed butter and sugar and stir them in. Finally add the syrup and stem ginger and stir until combined.

3 Divide mixture into 16 and roll into balls about the size of a walnut in its shell. Put them on to the lined baking tray and press down lightly with the palm of your hand, leaving a gap of about two fingers (at least an inch) between them to allow for spreading while in the oven. Bake for 12 minutes until golden. Leave to cool on the tray for 15 minutes.

Tom's tip: These spread during cooking and the pieces of stem ginger will stand proud of the finished biscuits. This adds to the deliciousness, in my view!

TEA-SOAKED DRIED FRUIT
··· FILLS A 1-LITRE KILNER JAR ···

Excellent for when fresh fruit isn't freely available. In fact, useful to have on hand at any time. Serve with yogurt and oat crunch (see page 19) or just eat on its own first thing in the morning when you've got an early start. Apricots, figs, prunes and dried apple are all lush like this.

500g dried fruit of your choice	3 star anise	750ml water
4 Earl Grey teabags	a piece of lemon peel	
1 tbsp brown sugar	6 smashed cardamom pods	

1 Put the dried fruit in a 1-litre Kilner jar.

2 Put the remaining ingredients into a large teapot or heatproof jug. Bring the water to the boil and pour over the teabags and flavourings. Allow to brew for 3–5 minutes, then strain and pour over the fruit in the Kilner jar. Fasten the lid and leave for at least 24 hours. Once it's cool enough, keep it in the fridge.

Tom's tip: This keeps for a week in the fridge. We almost always have some on the go at home.

BRUNCH

HENRY

Brunch is great. It's all about time off: waking up naturally, getting up slowly, having a piece of toast to tide you over, then making yourself something proper to eat. It starts with great coffee – and our good friend and UK champion barista Maxwell is here to give you the definitive low-down on that – and moves on to sausages, coddles, all that kind of stuff. The whole day is open to you and anything seems possible. There's that moment at brunch where you just feel happy.

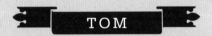

TOM

If a brunch could go on for four or five hours, and then at the end slide into dinner and involve wine, that would be a real treat. Like New Year's Day.

MAKING GREAT COFFEE AT HOME

MAKE YOUR OWN SAUSAGES:
CHIPOLATAS
PORK AND BLACK PUDDING
MEATY GARLIC SAUSAGE
WILD VENISON AND RED WINE
STRATFORD SAUSAGE

MARMITE PANCAKES

BLACKPOOL BREAKFAST

FLOURY BAPS

MUSHROOM KETCHUP

ARBROATH ARNOLD BENNETT OMELETTE

CODDLED EGGS WITH WILD MUSHROOMS AND LOVAGE

GREEN EGGS & HAM CODDLE

CHERRY AND PISTACHIO BREAKFAST TRIFLE

MAKING GREAT
COFFEE AT HOME

By Maxwell Colonna-Dashwood, owner of Colonna and Small's of Bath:
good friend, UK barista champion 2012, and rated sixth in the world

Coffee is an incredible drink, with many thousands of flavour components. Realizing its full flavour potential requires a bit of know-how.

The variety of coffee plant, the climate and the soil it grew in all contribute to the flavour that ends up in the cup, but it doesn't stop there. The coffee cherries need to be picked ripe and carefully processed. Then the green beans (the colour before roasting takes place) get shipped across the world and into the hands of a roaster. The roaster's job is to coax the character out of the bean using the application of heat. Get the roasting just right, and the beans will be bursting with aroma. If roasted too dark, then all you will taste is roasty, carbon-like flavours. At this point the coffee's flavour potential is close to being at its height, and time is now of the essence. Freshly roasted coffee changes from the moment it pops out of the roasting drum. The carbon dioxide present in the bean begins to leave, oxidation occurs and volatile flavour compounds begin to dissipate into the atmosphere. This is not to say that coffee is best straight after roasting, but you've got roughly one month to explore the flavour before too much has slipped away, regardless of how it is stored.

Now it's the turn of the maker –
whether barista or at-home drinker –

so it's worth getting this bit right. It's trickier than you might think. If everything else has been done well, the brewer can now release the flavour potential of the bean. At this point it all becomes about taste and recipe: the recipe dictates the taste and the taste informs the recipe.

When brewing coffee, we have our recipe variables: dose (amount of coffee), amount of water, time, grind size and water temperature.

The key concept that underpins all coffee brewing is the knowledge that flavours release themselves from the coffee and into the water in a particular order; it's not just a case of less or more 'coffee' flavour. First of all, the fruit acids give themselves up, followed by aromatic notes. Then we get the lovely caramels, and lastly we get the ashy burnt notes. We need some of these ashy notes to help provide balance, though too many will sully the cup.

Espresso is a wonderful way to brew, but filter coffee is the great under-appreciated marvel. In fact, the grading and blind assessment of the world's most revered coffees takes place in a format much closer to filter. Filter methods offer the opportunity to explore provenance and flavour at home. I am now going to go through a fantastic way to explore all this flavour that is just waiting to be enjoyed.

RELEASE
THE FLAVOUR

The Aeropress is a nifty piece of kit that allows for full immersion brewing and a clean, crisp cup, and I recommend it highly. It doesn't cost much, and you can buy them online.

You need fresh water that's not too hard. The ideal is 150 parts per million of minerals and other stuff in the water. At our store in Bath we need to filter the water a great deal as it's a rather high 350 parts per million. Volvic mineral water is a good starting point.

And you need some brilliant, freshly roasted coffee from a world-class roaster who focuses on provenance. Look for roast dates, farm names, plant varieties and processing methods on the bag. It's not really about the variety or process, it's transparency and traceability you're looking for. You will also need a burr grinder, some scales and a timer – and you are ready for the off!

1 Weigh out 15g coffee beans and set the grind to medium. Grind the coffee freshly for each cup, making sure you get 15g grounds at the end and that none of your dose is retained by the grinder.

2 Meanwhile, start the kettle boiling. You are looking for a temperature of around 94°C with lightly roasted coffee, and most domestic kettles should settle at around that temperature a minute after they have come off the boil. (Aeropress coffee makers break this rule a little and can make great coffee at lower temperatures.)

3 Rinse the Aeropress paper and sit it upside down and extended in the Aeropress.

4 Place the ground coffee in the top and add 220g of the off-the-boil water.

5 Set the timer for 1 minute; give the solution one stir with a suitable wooden implement to make sure all the coffee is immersed in the water and there are no dry lumps hanging about. Lock the top and the filter in place.

6 When your timer goes off, spin the Aeropress back around and sit it on top of your cup/receptacle (so it now has the filter at the bottom), and spend 30 seconds pushing all the way down on the Aeropress plunger, leaving your finished brew in the cup.

Now, you have taken a lot of care but your brew may not taste wonderful yet. You need to let the coffee cool down a little to taste it properly. At this point you can diagnose whether or not it's a good extraction. Depending on what you taste, you can change some of the variables to achieve the best possible coffee. This process is called dialling in.

TASTE
DIAGNOSTICS

It takes practice to understand the taste difference between over- and under-extraction. Sometimes it's not obvious; try tasting deliberate extremes of both to get a taste for it.

If the coffee tastes sharp, acidic and dry (in a furry-tongue kind of way) and makes you want a glass of water, then it is most likely under-extracted. Not enough flavour has been taken from the coffee to give us a balanced cup.

Consider temperature: use hotter water, by leaving it off the boil for only 45 seconds.

Or

Try changing your dose: take
the amount of coffee down by 0.5g
to give the water less flavour to
extract through.

Or

Try changing the brew time:
add 20 seconds to the immersion
stage to extract more flavour groups.

Or

Try a finer grind, allowing greater
surface area for more extraction.

If the coffee tastes flat, ashy and bland,
then this is over-extraction. You have
moved through too many flavour groups
and the roasty, ashy notes are hiding
all the interesting flavour.

Consider temperature: maybe the
water is too hot. Leave the kettle off the
boil for longer: try 1 minute 20 seconds.

Or

Try changing your dose: take the
amount of coffee up by 0.5g, providing
the water with more flavour to balance
the ashy notes.

Or

Try changing the brew time: take
15 seconds off the immersion stage
of the brewing process.

I hope you discover a whole new world
of coffee and flavour that makes your
brunch complete. Come and see us
when you're next in the south-west.

Maxwell Colonna

www.colonnaandsmalls.co.uk

MAKE YOUR OWN SAUSAGES

Ideally, make sausages the day before you want them so they can firm up in the fridge. You need casings – either hog or sheep, according to the recipe – which you can order online, or ask your butcher for them. You also need a sausage-stuffer to help you fill the casings, otherwise this is no fun at all and you might as well make patties or meatballs instead. Sausage-stuffers are inexpensive and well worth it, and once you've got one you can make sausages to freeze so you've always got a supply.

Once you've got the salty bundle of casings, grab a piece and yank it out, trying to loosen about 2 metres' worth, cut it, put it in cold water to soak, and put the rest back in the fridge, or freeze it. You are soaking the casings to wash the packing salt off and loosen them up; it takes about 5–10 minutes.

When you are ready to stuff the sausages, slip the casing on to the stuffing machine, leaving a 'tail' of about 15cm at the end of the tube. Put the meat in the top of the sausage-stuffer, and crank the handle to press the meat out. As soon as the meat appears at the end of the tube, tie off the tail – this is to avoid having air pockets in the sausage. If you tie too soon, you might end up with a sausage dog balloon. Then, using one hand to regulate how fast the casing slips off the tube, continue to fill the entire length. Don't overfill; have it well packed but not tight. Let the sausage come out in one long coil; you will make links later. You should have about 15cm of 'tail' left at the other end of the casing when you've finished.

With two hands, starting at the knotted end, pinch off and twist to make sausages of about 5 inches (12–13cm) long. Finally, knot the casing at the other end. Don't cut them yet, but leave the coil in the fridge to firm up, ideally for a day.

It is possible to make no end of lovely flavours. Really, it's liberty hall, but here a few of my favourites. Sausages freeze very well, so always make more than you need immediately.

PROPER COOKING

Never rush the cooking of a sausage or it will live up to its name and go BANG! If you cook it too quickly, the outside will split, the juice will run out and you will end up with a dry sausage. If you cook it in a pan, do so slowly on a low heat, turning every few minutes. A nice thick sausage will take around 20 minutes to cook through. However, my preferred method is to poach the sausage for 10 minutes in just simmering water. This will gently cook the sausage without much loss of moisture. Then remove the poached sausage, dab dry and finish off in a hot pan to crisp the outside. This method also works very well if you're doing a barbecue, as you can finish the sausages outside very quickly and with total confidence that they are cooked through and not burnt.

CHIPOLATAS

··· MAKES 25 ···

This is the thin, mild breakfast sausage that cooks quickly. It's a very British sausage, but its name comes from the Italian 'cipollata', meaning something flavoured with onion. However, there is no onion in a British chipolata! It's something we adopted and adapted so much that it bears no relation to its original inspiration, only the name remains. I always have these as part of a cooked breakfast as I find highly flavoured ones can be too much in the morning. These are filled into sheep casings, which makes them thinner than hog casings, which is why you get more sausages out of this recipe than the others.

2kg lean pork mince (shoulder)	1 tsp ground white pepper	200ml cold water
500g fatty pork mince (belly)	few grinds of nutmeg	sheep casings, soaked (see page 33)
1 tbsp caster sugar or honey	40g fine sea salt	
1 tsp ground coriander	100g very dry breadcrumbs	

1 Put the pork mince with the sugar, seasonings and breadcrumbs in a bowl and mix well with your hands. When fully incorporated, add the water and give it a good stir to combine.

2 Slip the casing on to the stuffing machine, leaving a tail. Put the meat in the stuffer, and crank it out to fill the casing, tying off the tail when the first meat emerges. When the casing is full and the meat used up, twist into links and then tie off the other end. If this is your first time making sausages, see the more detailed instructions on page 33, where you'll also find the best way to cook them.

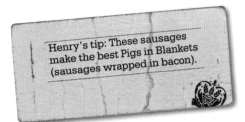

Henry's tip: These sausages make the best Pigs in Blankets (sausages wrapped in bacon).

PORK AND BLACK PUDDING

··· MAKES 20 ···

A herby sausage with big chunks of black pudding running through.
These meaty bangers will also pimp up any Toad in the Hole (see page 200).

2kg lean pork mince (shoulder)	1 tbsp chopped parsley	100g very dry breadcrumbs
500g fatty pork mince (belly)	1 pinch each of ground nutmeg and allspice	200ml cold water
1 garlic clove, grated		250g black pudding, skinned and diced into 1cm cubes
1 tsp thyme leaves	1 tsp cracked black pepper	
8 sage leaves, chopped	40g fine sea salt	hog casings, soaked (see page 33)

1 Put the pork mince with the garlic, herbs, seasoning and breadcrumbs in a bowl and mix well with your hands. When fully incorporated, add the water and give it a good stir to combine. Now stir through the black pudding dice.

2 Slip the casing on to the stuffing machine, leaving a tail. Put the meat in the stuffer, and crank it out to fill the casing, tying off the tail when the first meat emerges. When the casing is full and the meat used up, twist into links and then tie off the other end. If this is your first time making sausages, see the more detailed instructions on page 33, where you'll also find the best way to cook them.

Henry's tip: You add the black pudding to the sausage mixture at the end so it doesn't break up too much.

MEATY GARLIC
SAUSAGE

··· MAKES 20 ···

Henry: I quite often get asked for gluten-free sausages in the butchery,
so I've come up with this sausage that uses no breadcrumbs (or rusk, the
butcher's equivalent). It uses coarser mince – ask your butcher for it –
and makes for a really meaty sausage well suited to slow cooking.

2kg lean pork mince (shoulder, coarsely minced: ask your butcher)	5 garlic cloves, grated	hog casings, soaked (see page 33)
	1 tsp cracked black pepper	
	1 tsp ground nutmeg	
500g fatty pork mince (belly, coarsely minced: ask your butcher)	1 tsp thyme leaves	
	40g fine sea salt	
	100ml red wine	

1 Put the pork mince with the seasonings in a bowl and mix well with your hands. When well incorporated, add the red wine and mix thoroughly. It will be a looser, coarser mix than the others here, but this is the nature of the sausage.

2 Slip the casing on to the stuffing machine, leaving a tail. Put the meat in the stuffer, and crank it out to fill the casing, tying off the tail when the first meat emerges. When the casing is full and the meat used up, twist into links and then tie off the other end. If this is your first time making sausages, see the more detailed instructions on page 33, where you'll also find the best way to cook them.

WILD VENISON AND RED WINE

··· MAKES 20 ···

Dark rich venison meat with juniper and red wine gives these sausages balls.
If you find them too hard-core for brunch, serve on a huge pile of mash with
onion gravy for dinner – now we're talking!

1kg lean pork mince (shoulder)	1 small red chilli, diced	1 tsp chopped thyme
1kg venison mince	1 tsp cracked black pepper	100g very dry breadcrumbs
500g fatty pork mince (belly)	1 tsp ground mace	100ml red wine
40g fine sea salt	1 tsp ground juniper	100ml cold water
1 tbsp honey	pinch of cayenne pepper	hog casings, soaked (see page 33)
1 garlic clove, grated	1 tsp chopped rosemary	

1 Put the pork and venison mince with the seasonings and breadcrumbs in a bowl and mix well with your hands. When fully incorporated, add the wine and water and mix again.

2 Slip the casing on to the stuffing machine, leaving a tail. Put the meat in the stuffer, and crank it out to fill the casing, tying off the tail when the first meat emerges. When the casing is full and the meat used up, twist into links and then tie off the other end. If this is your first time making sausages, see the more detailed instructions on page 33, where you'll also find the best way to cook them.

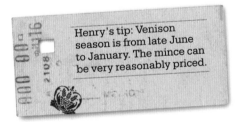

Henry's tip: Venison season is from late June to January. The mince can be very reasonably priced.

STRATFORD SAUSAGE

··· SERVES 20 AT A PARTY ···

This was done out of the back of the van, as we introduced ourselves to the people of Stratford-upon-Avon. The town's Tudor history inspired the spices and sherry. When you make sausages at home, take advantage of the fridge and chill the coil of links overnight so they are easier to cut up and fry the next day. Serve with the Marmite pancakes on page 41. The quantities make a tasty handful per person.

FOR THE SPICED SAUSAGE:

2kg lean pork mince
(shoulder, coarsely minced:
ask your butcher)

500g fatty pork mince
(belly, coarsely minced:
ask your butcher)

40g fine sea salt

2 tsp chopped fresh sage

1 tsp fresh thyme leaves

1 tsp cracked black pepper

good pinch of mace

good pinch of ginger

100g very dry breadcrumbs

1 generous tbsp honey

2 garlic cloves, chopped

100ml dry sherry

rapeseed oil, for frying

FOR THE GLAZE:

1 tbsp wholegrain mustard

3 tbsp honey

1 To make the sausages, place the coarsely ground meat and fat in a bowl. Add the rest of the ingredients, except the sherry and oil, and mix well with your hands. Then add the sherry and mix well to combine.

2 Follow the instructions for sausage stuffing on page 33. When you've extruded all the meat from the sausage-stuffer, start at the knotted end of the filled casings and pinch off and twist what will become small sausages, about 5cm long (or long sausages about 12cm). You should get about 40 cocktail sausages or about 20 of the longer ones. Finally, tie a knot in the other end and put in the fridge overnight to firm up.

3 To make the glaze, mix the mustard and honey together.

4 Cut through the links to separate the sausages. Heat the oil in a frying pan, add the sausages and cook gently, turning from time to time, for 4–5 minutes until golden all over. Add the glaze and cook for a further 3 minutes. Serve with Marmite pancakes.

MARMITE PANCAKES

··· MAKES ABOUT 20 SMALL PANCAKES ···

Marmite pancakes are a revelation – everyone loves them.

250g self-raising flour	100ml milk	a jar of onion chutney (optional), to serve
2 free-range eggs	40g butter, for frying	
1 tbsp Marmite		

1 To make the pancakes, put the flour into a bowl, break in the eggs, then add the Marmite and milk and whisk. Mix to a smooth but quite thick batter (like drop scones).

2 Heat a frying pan, add a little butter, then put in a serving spoon of batter (about 2 tbsp) and cook till golden and showing a few air bubbles. Turn over and cook the other side. About a minute and a half each side will do it. Each pancake should be about 6cm across. You can make a few at a time, depending on the size of your frying pan.

3 To serve: dollop a teaspoon of chutney, if using, on the pancake, add a couple of Stratford sausages (see page 38), fold the edges up and give to your companions – while you continue making pancakes.

BLACKPOOL BREAKFAST BAPS
··· SERVES 4 ···

Henry: Hashed potato is the unsung hero of the full English, and it really should be done well. We've taken the English hash – fried potato with onions, parsley and a bit of corned beef – and we've reimagined it, substituting black pudding for the corned beef, and putting it together in a big seeded bap with a fried egg to make the ultimate take-away breakfast. The only thing the people of Blackpool didn't like was the poppy-seed topping on the baps (see overleaf). The café owner told us, 'People up north don't like seeds. That's a southern thing.'

FOR THE HASH:

3 medium onions, sliced

knob of butter

750g potatoes, peeled (such as Maris Piper or King Edwards)

1 egg, beaten

100g black pudding, skinned and diced into 1cm cubes

small handful of flat-leaf parsley, chopped

juice of 1 lemon

1 tsp smoked paprika

salt and pepper, to taste

olive or rapeseed oil, for frying

TO FINISH:

4 floury baps (see page 46)

mushroom ketchup (see page 47)

1 fried egg per bun

3 slices of bacon per bun

1 To make the hash, slowly cook the onions in the butter until soft. Meanwhile, coarsely grate the potatoes into a clean tea towel and squeeze out the excess liquid by twisting the towel. You may need to do this a couple of times before the liquid stops coming out.

2 Put the potatoes and onions in a large bowl. Add the egg, black pudding, parsley, lemon juice, paprika and a good amount of salt and pepper. Mix the ingredients well.

3 Heat a good glug of oil in a heavy-based frying pan over a medium to high heat. When the oil is hot, add 2 large spoonfuls of the hash mix and flatten into patties about 3cm thick. Flip over once browned and crispy: about 5 minutes each side. Fry the eggs and bacon to your liking.

4 Slice the baps open, smear with mushroom ketchup, place the black pudding hash on top, then finish with fried egg and crispy bacon. Put the top on and serve at once.

FLOURY BAPS

··· MAKES 4 ···

Tom: Floury baps such as these are very simple to make. You can do them in a batch in a roasting tin, and there is nothing finer in the kingdom of bread-baking than the bit where the rolls are batched together: you pull them apart and right there is the softest bit of bread in the whole world. Whether you top them with seeds, of course, is up to you.

5g dried yeast	1 tsp caster sugar	1 egg, beaten
50ml tepid water	10g butter	poppy seeds, to sprinkle over (optional)
250g strong white flour, plus extra for dusting	5g sea salt	
	100ml tepid milk	

1 Stir the yeast into the tepid water and set aside to dissolve.

2 Weigh the flour, sugar, butter and salt into a large bowl and add the milk. Add the dissolved yeast and mix thoroughly into a dough. Turn it out on to a lightly floured surface and knead for 15 minutes until it is soft and elastic. Leave to rise for 1 hour in a covered bowl in a warm place.

3 Divide the dough into 4 and, on a lightly floured surface, roll into balls with the palms of your hands. Then, using a rolling pin, flatten them slightly. Place on a baking tray lined with baking paper. You don't need to leave much space around them; they can rise into one another.

4 Using a fine sieve, dust with flour for a traditional finish, or, if you're going shiny and seeded, brush beaten egg over each bap. Cover loosely with cling film and leave in a warm place for 30 minutes.

5 Brush with a second coat of beaten egg and sprinkle with a pinch of poppy seeds, if using, or finish them the Blackpool way with another dusting of flour. Cover loosely with cling film and leave for a final 30 minutes to rise.

6 Heat the oven to 200°C/Gas 6. Bake the baps until they are perfectly golden, about 12 minutes.

MUSHROOM KETCHUP

··· MAKES ABOUT 500G ···

This is an old-fashioned condiment. It's fallen out of favour, and we feel it's time to revive its popularity. When home-made, it's simply amazing, especially as an accompaniment to breakfast or brunch.

2 tbsp rapeseed oil	1 small bunch of thyme, leaves picked	½ tsp cayenne pepper
600g mushrooms (such as chestnut and Portobello), roughly chopped	3 garlic cloves, chopped	50ml sherry vinegar
	3 tbsp Worcestershire sauce	150ml water
		1 tbsp salt
2 onions, roughly chopped	150g brown sugar	black pepper

1 Put a large saucepan on a high heat, add the oil and, as soon as it is hot, add the mushrooms and fry until they release their liquid and it evaporates: about 10 minutes.

2 Turn down the heat and add the onions, thyme and garlic, and fry for a further 5 minutes.

3 Add the Worcestershire sauce, brown sugar, cayenne pepper, sherry vinegar, water, salt and pepper to taste, reduce the heat, cover and cook for a further 10–15 minutes. Let it cool a little.

4 Put the ketchup in a blender and purée till smooth. Put into a sterilized jar (see page 21), leave to cool completely and then refrigerate.

Henry's tip: Keeps in a jar in the fridge for up to 2 weeks. Totally awesome ketchup, and a worthy rival to the classic tomato (see page 21).

ARBROATH ARNOLD BENNETT OMELETTE

··· MAKES ENOUGH FOR 2–4, DEPENDING ON APPETITE ···

Henry: This is my take on the classic Arnold Bennett, a dish that will leave you wanting to do nothing but relax and enjoy life. I recommend only making it on a lazy weekend with no immediate plans ahead. The classic recipe calls for smoked haddock and hollandaise sauce, but I rather like this one.

1 large Arbroath smokie	250ml milk	40ml double cream
butter: 40g for the white sauce, plus 30g for cooking	3 tsp chopped parsley	handful of grated Parmesan
	salt and pepper	Dijon mustard, to serve (optional)
15g flour	6 eggs	

1 Pick the smokie into flakes. Try not to mash the fish too much, and keep an eye out for bones, which would not be so much fun in the omelette. In a small pan, melt 40g butter and add the flour. Beat until smooth, then slowly add the milk, beating all the while. This is to make a white sauce. When all the milk is in and the sauce is smooth and glossy, stir in the fish, chopped parsley and seasoning. Remove from the heat.

2 In a large, flameproof frying pan, melt 30g butter and add the eggs. Season and break up with a fork. Keep stirring with the fork over a gentle heat until the omelette has started to set: 1–2 minutes. Remove from the heat. Heat the grill to hot.

3 In a bowl whisk the double cream until thick, then fold it through the white sauce. Spoon the sauce over the omelette and sprinkle with Parmesan. Place under the grill for 2 minutes or until golden and bubbling. Spoon out and eat with a slick of Dijon mustard if you fancy. The perfect brunch.

Henry's tip: We watched the making of Arbroath Smokies in a demonstration at a food festival in Dundee. Eating a fresh, warm, smoky Smokie was mind-blowing. Totally worth seeking out if you haven't tried them before.

CODDLED EGGS WITH WILD MUSHROOMS AND LOVAGE

··· SERVES 4 ···

Henry: I love the sound of 'coddled egg'. It's so wonderfully warming and homely. And eating one is just as much of a pleasure. A coddle is a small ceramic pot that sits in a pan of gently simmering water. In the pot you put an egg and other accessories and gently poach or steam until cooked. The coddled egg has the texture of poached egg but with the addition of seasonings. I feel it is Britain's *oeuf cocotte* but so much better. Ask your grandmother for coddling pots, or use ramekins with a lid of tin foil.

100g or large handful of wild mushrooms, such as chanterelles or trompettes	salt and pepper	4 slices of bread, freshly toasted and buttered
	large pinch of chopped lovage or parsley	
1 tbsp butter, plus extra for greasing the pots	8 eggs	
	splash of double cream	

1 Tear the mushrooms into pieces if they are large. In a frying pan, heat the butter until foaming. Add the mushrooms, toss them around in the butter then fry them until they start to soften: about 2 minutes. Season and remove from the heat. Add the lovage and stir it through.

2 Grease the inside of 4 coddling pots or small ramekins and divide half the mushrooms between them. Crack 2 eggs into each one, and spoon the remaining mushrooms on top. Splash some cream on top and a pinch of seasoning.

3 Place the coddle pots or ramekins into a sauté pan of gently simmering water. Gently cook for 8 minutes or until the egg whites have just set.

4 Serve immediately with hot buttered toast.

GREEN EGGS
& HAM CODDLE
··· SERVES 4 ···

Henry: Dr Seuss and his Cat in the Hat was one of my favourite children's books. I loved the bonkersness of it all. Green eggs and ham always stuck with me as a crazy thing to eat. It got me thinking of how a delicious breakfast could be made using the name as inspiration.

20g butter, plus extra for greasing the pots	8 free-range fresh eggs (no green ones please)	**FOR THE HOLLANDAISE:**
200g spinach	100g hollandaise sauce	125g unsalted butter
half a lemon	8 slices of Parma ham	½ tsp white wine vinegar
salt, pepper and nutmeg	4 slices of bread, freshly toasted (optional)	1 egg yolk
		salt
		squeeze of lemon

1 First make the hollandaise. Melt the butter gently in a saucepan. In another pan, heat some water and place a bowl on top. Add the vinegar and egg yolk to the bowl, then whisk in a pinch of salt. Keep whisking over the heat until the yolk starts to thicken. Turn the heat down as low as it goes and slowly trickle in the melted butter, whisking all the time. It will gradually thicken, like a mayonnaise. Keep going until all the butter is in and you have a thick yellow sauce. Squeeze in a little lemon juice. Remove from the heat and cover to keep warm.

2 Heat a saucepan and add the butter. When it starts to sizzle, add the spinach. Cook for 2 minutes until it has started to wilt. Squeeze in a splash of lemon and season with salt, pepper and a grinding of nutmeg. Remove from the heat and set aside.

3 Butter the inside of 4 coddles or ramekins. Put half the spinach into the dishes. Crack 2 eggs in each one and top with the remaining spinach. Place the coddle pots or ramekins into a sauté pan of gently simmering water. Gently cook for 8 minutes or until the egg whites have just set.

4 Meanwhile, heat the grill. When hot, grill the Parma ham slices on a tray until crispy, then remove and set to one side.

5 To serve, spoon some warm hollandaise over the eggs and break the Parma ham into shards and scatter on top. Eat immediately.

CHERRY AND PISTACHIO BREAKFAST TRIFLE

··· SERVES 4 ···

We love puddings but it's really naughty to eat them first thing in the morning, though perhaps a dip into last night's crumble on the way to the milk is passable. This delightful brekkie has all the fun of a proper pud but without the insane sugar rush.

400g fresh British cherries or other soft fruit	30ml water	40g chopped pistachios
2 tbsp honey	400g thick Greek yogurt	
	200g oat crunch (see page 19)	

1 Leave 4 whole cherries on one side, and stone the rest. I use the 'squish and pull' method: squish the cherry with the heel of your hand, then pull out the stone. Place the stoned cherries in a small pan with the honey and water. Bring to the boil and simmer for 5 minutes, until the fruit has softened and the liquid is glossy and syrupy. This is the compote. Have a sneaky taste. It may need a tad more honey, depending on the fruit.

2 Remove from the heat and take half out. Using a hand-held blender, whiz up the remainder in the pan to make a rich cherry purée.

3 Take 4 individual glasses and spoon equal amounts of the cherry compote into each one. Add an eighth of the yogurt to each. Drizzle over some cherry purée. Sprinkle a layer of oat crunch and a scatter of pistachios on top. Repeat with the yogurt, purée and a generous topping of oat crunch and pistachios. Pop a cherry on top and feel good about yourself.

Henry's tip: Apricots are my next favourite fruit, paired with hazelnuts.

LUNCH

HENRY

If you've had an early breakfast and no brunch,
then you need something in the middle of the day
to get you through to dinner, something fresh
that's quite easy to make. Lunch is generally
on the healthy side for me.

TOM

Lunch can also be about having people over
for a meal that's less formal than dinner.

LONDON PEA-SOUPER

MACKEREL PITTA POCKETS

GUNPOWDER LAMB WITH ROTIS

BEETROOT-CURED SALMON

SHAKESPEARE'S CODPIECE

COCKNEY CRAYFISH

THE MELTER BELTER WITH SPELT LOAF

VIKING FLATBREADS

BRAISED LETTUCE, PEAS AND CHILLI SALAD

SUNDAY SALAD WITH HOT-SMOKED SALMON

ROAST CARROT, CORIANDER AND CHICKPEA SALAD

GRILLED SPROUTING BROCCOLI WITH HAZELNUT PASTE

CAESAR SALAD

SWEETCORN, WALNUT AND BULGUR SALAD

ROAST BEETROOT, LENTILS, GOAT'S CURD AND MINT SALAD

POACHED EGG, BACON AND CROUTON SALAD

CUCUMBER SOUP AND SALMON TARTARE

LONDON PEA-SOUPER

··· MAKES 6 ···

Tom: It's a long time since London has seen a real pea-souper, but a lot of visitors still expect London to be swathed in the fog it describes. I couldn't resist playing with the name.

5g dried yeast (or 10g fresh)	3 tbsp good quality olive oil	400ml hot chicken stock
300ml tepid water	1 onion, diced	4 tbsp crème fraîche with 2 tsp horseradish cream mixed in
560g strong white flour	1 garlic clove, chopped	
10g sea salt	pinch of paprika, plus extra to serve	small bunch of mint, roughly chopped (12–18 small leaves reserved)
20ml rapeseed oil, plus extra for rubbing on the dough	pinch of cayenne pepper	
FOR THE PEA SOUP:	pinch of smoked sea salt	juice of 1 lemon, zest of half
1 knob of butter	500g frozen garden peas	200g smoked eel fillets, to serve

1 Stir the yeast into the water with a fork. Weigh the flour and salt into a bowl and add the oil. Pour in the dissolved yeast and stir. Once it comes together into a dough, turn it out and knead for 15 minutes (10 minutes by machine) until smooth and elastic. Put back in the bowl, cover in cling film and leave in a warm place to double in size or for 1 hour (whichever is first).

2 Heat the oven to 240°C/Gas 9, and put in a baking sheet or stone to heat up. Divide the dough into 6 balls, roll under the palm of your hands into a good round shape, then cover with rapeseed oil and place in a baking tray. Cover the tin and leave it in a warm place to double in size or for 30 minutes (whichever is first).

3 Place a dish of water on the oven floor for the perfect crust. Bake the rolls for 10 minutes, then turn the temperature down to 230°C/Gas 8 and bake for a final 10 minutes until golden.

4 To make the soup, heat the butter and the oil in a large pan over medium heat. Add the onion and garlic and fry for 3 minutes or until soft and just colouring. Stir in the paprika, cayenne and smoked sea salt, then add the frozen peas and the hot chicken stock and bring to the boil. Cover and simmer for about 6 minutes or until the peas are just cooked. Take off the heat.

5 Slice the tops off the rolls and remove the inner crumb to make a bowl for the soup. Add the crumb to the soup with the crème fraîche, mint and lemon zest and juice. Blitz with a hand-held blender or add to a liquidizer and blend until smooth.

6 Pour a little oil inside the bread rolls and season them. Return to the oven for another 5 minutes to harden slightly. Pour the soup into the bread rolls and flake the smoked eel over the top. Serve with a dusting of paprika and the reserved mint leaves on top.

MACKEREL PITTA POCKETS
··· SERVES 4 ···

We made these tasty morsels for the people of Exmouth. Delicious pockets of joy, in which crunchy watercress salad and the strong flavours of mackerel and horseradish go together really well. We made them as finger food; this version is for full-size pittas. (If you want tiny pittas, take pieces of dough the size of a grape.)

4 fresh mackerel fillets

1 tbsp olive oil

20g butter

FOR THE PITTA BREAD:

5g dried yeast (or 10g fresh)

300ml tepid water

560g bread flour (we used local flour from Otterton Mill)

10g sea salt

30ml olive oil

FOR THE SALAD:

2 small English apples, skin on, cut into thin slices

100g watercress, thick stalks removed

lemon juice, to taste

extra virgin olive oil

salt and pepper

FOR THE HORSERADISH CREAM:

60g creamed horseradish

60g mayonnaise

2 tbsp clotted cream

juice of half a lemon

1 To make the pitta bread, dissolve the yeast in the water. Put the flour into a mixing bowl, add the yeast and water, and the salt. Knead by hand for 5 minutes. Add the olive oil and continue to knead for 10 minutes until all the oil is absorbed. Shape the dough into a ball, cover, and leave in a warm area until doubled in volume or for 30 minutes, whichever is first.

2 Take pieces of dough about 100g in weight, and roll out on a floured surface into a disc 3–5mm thick. Place a non-stick frying pan over a medium-high heat. Put one of the pittas in the pan, cover with a lid and leave for 2–3 minutes until it puffs up. Flip over and cook for another 2–3 minutes on the other side. Some will puff more than others. Serve warm. (You will have leftover pittas you can cool then freeze.)

3 For the salad, mix together the apple and watercress, add a squeeze of lemon juice and a good drizzle of olive oil, and season with salt and pepper.

4 For the horseradish cream, place all the ingredients in a bowl, whisk, season and set aside.

5 Heat the tablespoon of olive oil with the butter in a frying pan over a medium-high heat. When hot, add the mackerel fillets skin-side down and cook for 2 minutes, until the skin is crisp and golden. Reduce the heat slightly, turn each fillet over and cook for a further minute, until just cooked through.

6 Open the freshly made pitta breads, fill with salad, add some crispy mackerel and drizzle with horseradish cream.

GUNPOWDER LAMB
··· SERVES 6 ···

We loved York. It's such a jewel of a place, with so much history. One of its claims to fame is that Guy Fawkes was born there, and baptized in the church next to the minster. If you go from the Guy Fawkes pub down the old lanes you come to the Shambles, a beautifully preserved medieval street, which was once home to all the town's butchers and where the blood would run in streams down the gullies. You can still see butchers' hooks. So in York we wanted to do something with meat, but we also wanted to make it explosive, in a way Guy Fawkes might have approved of. This is cooked fast, has a good spicy kick, and there's a fiery salad to go with it.

FOR THE LAMB:

4 x 200g lamb neck fillet

1 tsp turmeric

1 finger-sized piece of cassia bark

1 tsp cumin seeds

1 tsp coriander seeds

1 tsp black pepper

1 dried red chilli, crumbled

2cm fresh root ginger, roughly chopped

1 garlic clove, peeled

a good pinch of sea salt

2 tbsp rapeseed oil

FOR THE INDIAN SALAD:

2 tbsp rapeseed oil

1 tsp black mustard seeds

4 carrots, grated

2 roasted red peppers (see Fire Peppers, page 152), flesh torn into strips

1 red onion, very finely sliced

a small bunch of coriander, leaves picked and chopped

1 green chilli, finely chopped

the juice of 1 lemon

sea salt and black pepper

TO FINISH:

4 rotis (see page 64)

plain yogurt, to serve

1 For the lamb, bash all the spices, ginger, garlic and salt in a pestle and mortar until you have a rough paste. Mix in the oil, pour over the lamb and leave to marinate while you get on with the rotis and the salad.

2 Make the rotis as shown in the recipe on page 64.

3 To make the salad, heat some oil in a pan and add the mustard seeds. Allow them to pop, then remove from the heat. Pour the mustard seeds and oil over the grated carrot, then add the red pepper, onions, coriander, green chilli and lemon juice and mix well.

4 Heat a griddle pan until smoking hot and then griddle the lamb for 4 minutes on each side, turning from time to time. Slice or shred the lamb. Fill each roti with lamb, salad and yogurt, fold in half and serve at once.

ROTIS

··· MAKES 6 ···

Rotis are very easy to make and the classic thing to serve with a curry. There is a fine tradition of British Indian food in this country, though the ubiquitous 'curry' is one of those cooking styles we borrowed, then adapted, to the point where the original source no longer recognizes it. To go with any curry, a roti fresh out of the frying pan is delicious, and quicker than cooking rice. These are also the perfect accompaniment to Gunpowder Lamb, page 60.

300g self-raising flour	2 tsp black onion seeds	good glug of vegetable oil, plus extra for frying and brushing
½ tsp sea salt	1 tsp crushed dried chilli	
1 tsp cumin seeds		150ml warm water

1 Mix the flour and salt, cumin, onion seeds and dried chilli in a large bowl. Add the oil and enough water to make a soft, but not sticky, dough. Add a little more flour or water if needed. Knead gently until smooth. Cover and leave to rest for 5 minutes.

2 Divide the dough into 6 equal pieces and roll each one into a thin circle about the thickness of a 20-pence piece.

3 Heat a little oil in a heavy-based pan. Roll one of the roti thinly into a round with a rolling pin, and fry on one side until it puffs up and is speckled brown on the underside. Turn it over and fry on the other side for 30 seconds, until it too is puffed up and speckled brown. Lift up from the pan using metal tongs, allow the oil to drain off and then hold over an open flame until burnished. Allow the roti to cool for a few seconds, then wrap in a clean tea towel while you make the rest.

Henry's tip: Rotis don't last long once cooked, so make only the amount you need. The dough will keep for a week in the fridge.

BEETROOT-CURED SALMON

··· SERVES ABOUT 8 ···

The colour of this salmon really grabs the attention. Its stained flesh is a vivid purple fading to a rich orange with speckles of green. Not only is it incredibly simple to make, it tastes even better than it looks. It is lovely with soda or wheaten bread, horseradish and pickles.

1 side of organic salmon	20g black pepper	2 bunches of chopped dill:
200g sea salt	4 cooked beetroots,	1 bunch for the cure,
400g caster sugar	mashed	1 for garnish

1 Run your palm over the salmon flesh, against the grain, to feel for any pin bones that might be left in. Take them out with tweezers, then put the salmon, skin-side down, into a large dish or tray (plastic would be fine). Mix the salt, sugar, pepper, beetroot and dill to form a paste and rub all over the fish, making sure it's well covered. Pack the remaining mixture over the top and cover with cling film.

2 Place in the fridge and allow to cure for 2 days. Give it a turn a day. When the salmon is feeling firmer but not too dry, take it out of the container and brush off the salt paste. Chop up the second bunch of dill and pat on to the salmon flesh. This makes it look beautiful. Using a sharp thin knife, carefully slice into strips, as thinly as possible. Think of yourself as a Spanish serrano ham master. Use the leathery skin to keep the salmon in one piece. Don't try to eat the skin – it's not so good.

SHAKESPEARE'S CODPIECE

··· MAKES 4 ···

The Tudors liked to combine meats with sweets, and made the most of the exotic and precious spices that were available to them. Here we put our spin on this tradition: a good local pig, with ginger and spices in a fine filo pastry, and a dusting of icing sugar on top. A delicious parcel of porky joy. This is a really good summer dish, and one that lends itself to feeding a lot of people at a time.

FOR THE PULLED PORK:

2kg pork shoulder on the bone or 1.2kg boneless

1 onion, chopped

1 bulb of garlic, halved

2 tsp black peppercorns

1 tsp sea salt

10 whole cloves

1 cinnamon stick

½ tsp ground ginger

500ml cider

TO MAKE THE FILLING:

2 tbsp olive oil

3 onions, chopped

3cm fresh root ginger, grated

½ tsp ground cloves

1 tsp ground cinnamon

salt and pepper

pulled pork from above

200ml cooking juices from above

a few sprigs of parsley and sage, finely chopped

150g flaked almonds, toasted and roughly crushed

16 sheets filo pastry

80g unsalted butter, melted, plus extra for greasing

icing sugar and paprika, for dusting

1 Heat the oven to 150°C/Gas 2. Put the pork, onion and garlic into a large roasting tray. Bash the pepper, salt, cloves, cinnamon and ginger in a pestle and mortar, then rub into the pork. Pour the cider into the tray, taking care not to wash off the rub. Cover with foil and roast for 3 hours. Remove the foil and roast for another hour. Take out of the oven and let it sit for 15 minutes or so. 'Pull' the pork by shredding it into small pieces with a fork. Set aside with the cooking juices.

2 Heat the oven to 180°C/Gas 4. Put in a baking stone or tray to heat up.

3 To make the pork filling, heat the oil in a large frying pan and fry the onions for 6–8 minutes, until softened and slightly golden. Stir in the ginger, cloves and cinnamon, and season. Add the pulled pork to the pan along with the cooking juices, bring the mixture to the boil, then reduce the heat and simmer for 30 minutes, adding more water if the mixture looks dry. Add the parsley, sage and almonds to the pan and cook over a gentle heat for 4–5 minutes. Allow to cool for 30 minutes.

4 Lay 2 sheets of filo on the worktop and brush with melted butter. Add another 2 sheets and brush again. Spoon a quarter of the filling into the centre. Fold the pastry on top to form a kind of Elizabethan ruff, and brush with more melted butter. Place on a baking tray.

5 Bake for 25 minutes, or until the pastry is crisp and golden-brown on top. Sprinkle with icing sugar and paprika, and serve warm.

COCKNEY CRAYFISH

··· MAKES 12 CRAYFISH BOATS ···

Unless you catch your own crayfish, it's best and easiest to use the cooked, brined crayfish you can buy in tubs from the fishmonger or deli. This recipe was how we introduced ourselves to the people around the Tower of London.

2 tbsp extra virgin olive oil, plus extra for drizzling	sea salt and pepper	juice of 1 lemon
good pinch of smoked paprika	400g cooked, chopped crayfish in brine	a small bunch of dill
half a red chilli, finely chopped	a splash of good London gin	1 punnet of cress
4 shallots, finely sliced	3 tbsp crème fraîche	4 baby gem lettuces, trimmed
		zest of 1 lemon, to serve

1 Heat the olive oil in a large frying pan over a medium-high heat, then chuck in the paprika, red chilli and shallots, and salt and pepper to taste. Fry for 3 minutes until the shallots are just golden. Add the crayfish and gin and fry for a further 1–2 minutes. Stir in the crème fraîche, then pour the mixture straight from the pan into a bowl. Add the lemon juice, dill and cress. Give it a good mix and set aside.

2 Carefully remove the leaves of the baby gem one by one until you have 12 firm, good-sized specimens. Divide the crayfish mixture equally between the leaves, sprinkle over the lemon zest and drizzle with a little extra oil. Serve immediately.

Henry's tip: These make great party food. Add a G&T and you're off.

SPELT LOAF

··· MAKES 1 LARGE LOAF ···

Tom: Spelt is an ancient variety of wheat. It makes a loaf of substance, with a beautiful, nutty flavour, and it has become popular over the last fifteen years or so because it seems to be easier to digest for a lot of people – or so my customers say. It's a bestseller in Hobbs House.

FOR THE SPELT LOAF:	250g wholemeal spelt flour	10g fine-grain sea salt
5g dried yeast (or 10g fresh)	250g strong white bread flour, plus extra for dusting	
300ml tepid water		

1 Mix the yeast and tepid water until the yeast has dissolved. Combine the flours in a bowl, add the dissolved yeast and the salt, and bring together into a raggedy dough. Tip it out on to the work surface and knead vigorously for 15 minutes to make a soft, stretchy dough. Your dough will now be elastic, but not so elastic as regular wheat dough. Transfer to a bowl and cover it. Allow to prove until doubled in size (no more than 1 hour), in a warm place.

2 Grease a large (2lb) loaf tin. Once the dough has proved, shape it into a firm ball between cupped hands, then place it on the work surface and gently roll with the flat of your hands until it is the length of the tin. Place it in the tin, cover and leave to prove for a further hour or until doubled in size.

3 Heat the oven to 230°C/Gas 8. If you have one, put a baking stone into the oven to heat up at the same time.

4 Sprinkle the loaf with spelt flour and sea salt and transfer to the hot oven (to the stone, if using). Spray the oven with water spray and close the door to create a crust. Bake for 30 minutes. Remove the loaf from the oven, take out of the tin and leave to cool completely.

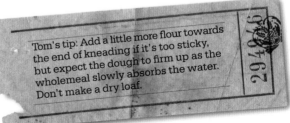

Tom's tip: Add a little more flour towards the end of kneading if it's too sticky, but expect the dough to firm up as the wholemeal slowly absorbs the water. Don't make a dry loaf.

THE MELTER BELTER

··· MAKES 4 ···

In Stratford we had great fun delving into the history of Tudor England and discovering the kind of food Shakespeare might have eaten (see Shakespeare's Codpiece on page 66, too). Here the combination of beef with good cheese and various condiments melting into it, and spelt bread holding it all together, was a winner. It was the winner, in fact. The beef, the cheese, the Worcestershire sauce – these are good Midlands ingredients. We recommend you enjoy this with a tankard of good local ale, just as Falstaff might have done.

1.5kg piece of beef brisket	1 tbsp juniper berries	50g brown sugar
FOR THE MARINADE:	1 tsp whole allspice	**TO ASSEMBLE:**
150g brown sugar	**FOR THE WORCESTERSHIRE ONIONS:**	8 slices of spelt bread (see page 68)
50ml Worcestershire sauce	1 tbsp butter	
1 tsp salt	2 tbsp olive oil	Butter
2 tsp black peppercorns, crushed	8 onions, sliced	English mustard
	3 tbsp Worcestershire sauce	Red Leicester cheese, sliced

1 To make the marinade, put all the ingredients into a bowl and mix together; then rub all over the beef brisket and leave to marinate overnight.

2 The next day, heat the oven to 150°C/Gas 2. Put the brisket in a large roasting tin, cover the tray with foil and roast for 3 hours, basting from time to time. Remove the foil and cook for a further 30 minutes to give it some colour.

3 To make the onions, heat the butter and olive oil in a large pan on a low heat, add the onions and cook for 5 minutes until softened. Add the Worcestershire sauce and sugar and continue to cook over a low heat for 10–15 minutes or until syrupy.

4 To assemble the sandwich, butter the bread on both sides. Spread over English mustard, followed by the sliced beef, some of the onions and slices of cheese. Pan-fry the sandwich till the bread has a nice browned colour and is crispy, then finish in the oven at 200°C/Gas 6 for 5 minutes till the cheese is melting. Serve warm.

Henry's tip: For added unctuousness, slice the beef and bathe it in the delicious meat juices before making the sandwich.

VIKING FLATBREADS

··· MAKES 8 ···

Tom: This is possibly my favourite recipe from the second television series.
The Vikings settled over here and cultivated and milled their own spelt. The
moment the historical re-enactment group told us that the Vikings used to make
a spelt flatbread with toppings, like an early pizza, I got the bit between my teeth
and had to run with it. If you wish to indulge your inner Viking, and you feel it
wouldn't be neighbourly to pillage the next village, making flatbreads might
be a better use of your energy and time. Good for vegetarians too.

5g dried yeast (or 10g fresh)	500g wholemeal spelt flour	for the topping ingredients, see overleaf
260ml tepid water	1 tsp sea salt	
a small handful of hazelnuts, toasted	50ml rapeseed oil, plus more for proving and topping	

1 Dissolve the yeast in the tepid water. Put the toasted nuts inside a folded-over tea towel and crush to a powder with a rolling pin. Put into a mixing bowl with the flour and salt, then stir in the yeast and water and bring it all together into a raggedy dough. Turn out and knead on the work surface until you have a very soft and stretchy dough: about 15 minutes by hand (10–12 minutes with a mixer). It's important not to shirk on the kneading. You want to get an elastic, super-stretchy dough that is robust and will give you great flatbreads. Put the dough back into the mixing bowl, cover and leave in a warm place for 1 hour.

2 Tip the dough on to a clean, flat work surface and divide into 8 equal pieces. Then make a claw from your hand and, using a circular action and a bit of palm pressure, mould the pieces into tight round rolls.

3 Slosh the rapeseed oil into a big roasting tin and roll the dough balls around, coating them with oil. This will stop them sticking to each other as they prove, and give the base a lush crust. Cover the tin and leave in a warm place to rise for an hour or so.

4 Meanwhile, fire your oven up as hot as it'll go with a baking stone or baking sheet in place. Anything above 230°C/gas mark 8 will work but 350–400°C in a wood-fired oven would be perfect, if this means of cooking is available to you. With the flatbreads proving and the oven heating up, prepare the topping (see overleaf).

5 To assemble, throw the dough into a rough circle then brush with rapeseed oil, spoon on the topping and bake in the super-hot oven for 4–5 minutes. Remove from the oven, drizzle with the marjoram oil and eat as soon as they are cool enough to handle.

TOPPING FOR THE VIKING FLATBREADS

··· SERVES 8 ···

You can make this with greens you find growing in the wild as the Vikings would have done, such as sorrel, which has a delicious lemony tartness. Spinach with nutmeg is also really good. Making your own curd cheese is what the Vikings would have done, but it's acceptable to buy it ready-made. This is healthy, good-looking and great-tasting.

2 big red onions, sliced

2 tbsp rapeseed oil

200g spinach or sorrel, chopped

a good grating of nutmeg if you are using spinach

200g curd cheese or ricotta

FOR THE MARJORAM OIL:

a few sprigs of marjoram, leaves picked

a garlic clove, roughly chopped

a good pinch of sea salt

2 tbsp rapeseed oil

1 Fry the onions in the oil slow and low until soft and sweet: about 15 minutes. Then stir in the spinach and nutmeg, or sorrel, and set aside.

2 To make the marjoram oil, crush the marjoram with the garlic and salt in a pestle and mortar (or under the flat of a knife blade on a chopping board) until combined into a paste. Add the oil and mix in. Set aside.

3 Use to top the Viking flatbreads (see page 72).

Tom's tip: The marjoram oil is amazingly delicious, will keep well for several days and can be drizzled over any breads or salads, as you like. So it might be worth making extra.

29476

BRAISED LETTUCE, PEAS AND CHILLI SALAD

··· SERVES 4–6 ···

This simple but delicious salad shows how versatile lettuce can be. Grilling or frying lettuce is such a good thing to do and transforms it totally.

1 mild red chilli, diced	2 cos lettuces, chopped	1 lemon
2 tbsp extra virgin olive oil	500g peas, fresh or defrosted from frozen	salt and pepper
2 garlic cloves, chopped		

1 Gently fry the chilli in the olive oil in a wide frying pan. After 2 minutes, add the garlic and lettuce, and cook until wilted: around 3 minutes.

2 Add the peas, stir and warm through. Dress with lemon juice and salt and pepper. Serve warm or cold.

Henry's tip: This is perfect with poached fish or grilled lamb chops.

SUNDAY SALAD
··· SERVES 6 ···

Henry: The perfect salad for a Sunday lunch, with an eye to a huge roast later on. The salad cream is old school. Some include a boiled yolk in the mix but I find that for the smoked salmon it's too eggy. The hot-smoked salmon (see overleaf) can be made in advance, and will keep for 5 days in the fridge.

FOR THE SALAD:		FOR THE SALAD CREAM:
2 baby gem lettuces cut into eighths, with the core removed	small bunch of dill, coarsely picked	100ml single cream
1 fennel, very thinly sliced	splash of virgin olive oil	1 tsp English mustard
1 tsp capers	squeeze of lemon	1 tbsp white wine vinegar
2 radishes, thinly sliced	salt and pepper	1 tsp sugar
	hot-smoked salmon (page 78)	salt and pepper

1 To make the salad cream, whisk all the ingredients together in a bowl. The cream will thicken naturally when mixed with the vinegar. If it goes too thick, a trickle of water will sort it out.

2 To serve, first mix the gem, fennel, capers, radishes and dill in a bowl and toss with the olive oil and lemon. Season with salt and pepper.

3 Build the salad on individual plates or a serving dish. Flake the salmon into healthy chunks over the salad. Either dollop the salad cream over or serve in a jug next to the salad.

HOT-SMOKED SALMON
··· MAKES 250G ···

Henry: Hot-smoking the salmon is quick, easy and will certainly set the fire alarm off. Open all the windows and whack the extraction fan up. Hot-smoked salmon keeps for 5 days in the fridge.

250g salmon fillet, wild or organic farmed	1 tsp brown sugar	**KIT:**
FOR THE CURE:	**FOR THE SMOKE:**	tin foil
½ tsp salt	50g rice	2 similar-sized deep metal trays
½ tsp pepper	30g camomile or green tea	a wire rack to position between the trays
	40g brown sugar	

1 Combine the cure ingredients and sprinkle the mix on to the salmon fillet. Place in the fridge for at least 1 hour to start curing. This seasons the fish and firms up the texture.

2 Now for the fun bit. Put tin foil in the bottom of one of the metal trays. Mix the rice, tea and sugar for the smoke, and sprinkle on the foil. Put the tray on the hob and turn the heat up. Place the salmon skin-side down on the wire rack and balance it on top of the metal tray. As the tray heats up, the mixture will start to smoke. As soon as it starts to smoke, turn the heat down. We want just a gentle smoke. Place the other metal tray upside down on top. This makes a box for the smoke to circulate in and cook the fish.

3 I like my salmon to be slightly underdone, which means smoking it for 8 minutes. Do it for 12 minutes if you prefer it more cooked. It is ready when you can flake the flesh easily. It should be juicy and shiny. Use a palette knife to lift the salmon on to a plate, and put in the fridge for 20 minutes to chill. This will keep for 5 days in the fridge.

ROAST CARROT, CORIANDER AND CHICKPEA SALAD
··· SERVES 4–6 ···

Roasted orange carrots, chalky chickpeas and fragrant coriander make
for a beautiful combination. This is a great vegetarian dish on its own,
and for meat-eaters it is very good with grilled lamb. This is the kind of
salad that is perfect when it's just warm; then the flavours really sing.

6 carrots, chopped into chunks	1 large bunch fresh coriander, leaves picked	**FOR THE DRESSING:**
2 tbsp olive oil		2 tbsp tahini (sesame-seed paste)
salt and pepper	1 tbsp sesame seeds	juice of 1 lemon
400g tin chickpeas		3 tbsp extra virgin olive oil

1 Heat the oven to 200°C/Gas 6.
Put the carrots in a roasting tin,
add the oil, season, and stir with your
hands so the carrots are well coated.
Roast for 30 minutes until the carrots
have lots of lovely colour and are tender.

2 Remove from the oven and stir in
the chickpeas. The residual heat
will warm the chickpeas through.
Chop the coriander and mix through
the salad with the sesame seeds.
Transfer to a large salad bowl.

3 Whisk the tahini, lemon juice
and olive oil in a small bowl,
then drizzle over the warm salad.

GRILLED SPROUTING BROCCOLI WITH HAZELNUT DRESSING

··· SERVES 4–6 ···

Henry: This is so simple and totally delicious; it's very good on its own or with grilled sausages, chicken or salmon. Sprouting broccoli (a.k.a. purple sprouting broccoli or PSB) is similar to the standard broccoli but I like it so much more. Maybe it is the mushy boiled broccoli at school that tainted my view.

50g hazelnuts	30ml extra virgin olive oil	
2 garlic cloves	salt and pepper	
small bunch of parsley, leaves picked	12 stems of sprouting broccoli	

1 First make the hazelnut dressing. Start by roasting the nuts in a dry pan for a few minutes until they are toasty and glistening. Pour straight into a pestle and mortar or food processor along with the garlic and grind up to a fine paste. Finely chop the parsley and mix through with the olive oil. Season. It will taste better still after a short while. Set to one side.

2 Heat a pan of water. When boiling, add the broccoli and boil for 4 minutes or until tender. Remove and reserve. This is fine, but to make it really good, heat a griddle pan and, when hot, add the drained cooked broccoli and char it for a few minutes. Place on a plate and spoon over the hazelnut dressing.

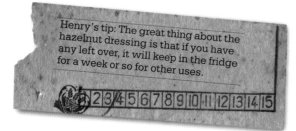

Henry's tip: The great thing about the hazelnut dressing is that if you have any left over, it will keep in the fridge for a week or so for other uses.

CAESAR SALAD

··· SERVES 4–6 ···

Henry: This is not a British dish, but it's ubiquitous here. It seems we've annexed it. And if we're going to do it, it deserves to be done well. This is how good it can be. I serve mine with grilled beef skirt in a steak sandwich. It just works.

2 slices good white bread	small block of Parmesan	20g grated Parmesan
20ml olive oil	**FOR THE DRESSING:**	squeeze of lemon
salt and pepper	2 garlic cloves	50ml olive oil
1 romaine lettuce or 2 baby gem lettuces	3 salted anchovy fillets	50ml vegetable oil
	1 egg yolk	salt and pepper

1 Cut the crusts off the bread and cut into small squares. Drizzle with oil and season. Heat a small frying pan and gently fry until brown and crunchy. If any burn, discard them.

2 To make the dressing, take a round-based bowl. Crush the garlic, chop up the anchovy, and add these with the egg yolk and grated Parmesan to the bowl. Squeeze in the lemon and whisk together.

3 Very slowly, drip by drip, whisk in the oils. We are making a mayonnaise-style dressing, so we want the sauce to thicken. If you add the oil too fast it may split. When all the oil is added, taste the dressing. It might need a little salt and pepper or another squeeze of lemon. If it's a little thick, whisk in a touch of cold water to loosen.

4 Cut the lettuce into largish strips and mix in a bowl with the dressing. Toss in the croutons and finish by shaving a few strips of Parmesan with a peeler on top.

Henry's tip: If the dressing splits, take another egg yolk in a clean bowl, squeeze in a touch of lemon and whisk the split dressing into the new yolk. You will need to use extra oil, and of course you will end up with more dressing than originally planned. I sometimes find that when it splits it keeps happening just to enrage you. Keep cool and remember that leftover dressing will keep in the fridge very well for a few days.

SWEETCORN, WALNUT AND BULGUR SALAD
··· SERVES 4–6 ···

Henry: Here I've taken inspiration from tabbouleh, my favourite Middle Eastern dish, and paired it with good old British corn. Sweetcorn tend to gets a rough ride, and I think this is unfair. It's a wonderful ingredient: succulent, sweet and delicious. Eat this with grilled meats or fish, or as a main-course salad.

3 corns on the cob, or 1 tin of sweetcorn kernels	500ml boiling water	**FOR THE DRESSING:**
1 tsp oil	50g walnuts, toasted	3 tbsp walnut oil
salt and pepper	large bunch of flat-leaf parsley, leaves picked	1 tbsp sherry vinegar
200g bulgur wheat	a pinch of dried chilli flakes	1 tsp honey
		1 garlic clove, crushed

1 If using corn on the cob, heat a dry griddle pan. Remove the outside leaves of the corn. Rub with a little oil and season. Place on the hot griddle pan and cook for 10 minutes, turning frequently until you have charred, cooked corn, ready to eat. Remove from the grill and allow to cool for 5 minutes before handling. When cool enough, run the blade of a knife down the length of the cob, cutting off just the corn, leaving the core/husk behind. Place the corn into a salad bowl.

2 If using tinned sweet corn – it will not be quite as good but still nice – drain the tin and fry the corn in a frying pan in a little oil for 5 minutes until the kernels have some colour.

3 Put the bulgur wheat in a bowl with a pinch of salt and the boiling water, cover with a tea towel and leave for 30 minutes for the wheat to absorb the liquid and swell. Remove the towel and, using a fork, gently rough up the wheat, letting the steam out. When cool, add to the corn.

4 Crush the toasted walnuts and chop the parsley. Add to the salad, along with the dried chilli.

5 To make the dressing, mix all the ingredients together in a small bowl and pour over the salad. Give it a thorough toss and serve.

ROAST BEETROOT, PUY LENTILS, GOAT'S CURD AND MINT SALAD

··· SERVES 4–6 ···

We love the autumnal feel of this salad, the deep purple and brown colours and the reassuring creaminess of the curd. Hot or cold, this salad is lush.

6 baby beetroots	200g Puy lentils	2 tbsp virgin olive oil
splash of olive oil	500ml water or vegetable stock	1 tbsp sherry vinegar
salt and pepper	2 shallots	100g goat's curd (use soft goat's cheese if you can't find curd)
2 sprigs of thyme	small bunch of mint, leaves picked	

1 Heat the oven to 150°C/Gas 3. Toss the beetroot with oil, salt and pepper and 1 sprig of thyme. Wrap in tin foil, put on a baking tray and roast in the oven for around 45 minutes to an hour. To check they are done, pierce the foil and beets with a small knife. If it goes in easy, remove the beets and allow to cool for 10 minutes. Then, while still hot, rub the skins off – rubber gloves are a good idea here – to leave you with 6 shiny purple orbs. Cut into quarters and leave to one side.

2 Put the lentils in a pan, cover with stock or water, add the other thyme sprig and bring to the boil. The lentils will take around 25 minutes to cook. When tender, season and drain off any excess liquid. Pour on to a tray and spread evenly so the lentils can cool quickly.

3 Slice the shallots thinly and chop the mint. Mix the beetroot, lentils, shallot and mint together, season and dress with the oil and vinegar. Divide between plates and dot with goat's curd.

POACHED EGG, BACON AND CROUTON SALAD

··· SERVES 2 ···

Texture, temperature and flavour play a big part in marrying these simple ingredients into a great salad. It's the salad form of the egg and bacon sandwich.

2 slices good white bread	salt and pepper	1 tsp wholegrain mustard
40ml extra virgin olive oil	1 small frisée lettuce	white wine vinegar to poach the eggs
1 garlic clove, crushed	1 bunch of watercress	
sprig of rosemary, roughly chopped	30g thick-cut bacon, chopped	2 free-range eggs
	1 tbsp red vinegar	1 tsp chopped chives

1 Cut the crusts off the bread and cut into small squares. Heat a small frying pan and add half the oil, the garlic and the rosemary. Toss in the bread and season. Cook gently until golden brown and super crunchy. Remove and drain excess oil on a paper towel.

2 Discard the green outer leaves of the frisée, which can be excessively bitter. Cut the inner leaves and put into a big bowl. Chop the stalks off the watercress and mix with the frisée.

3 Using the crouton pan, reheat it and gently fry the bacon. The fat will render out and stop them from burning. When they are nice and crispy, pour in the vinegar and mustard, turn off the heat and toss together.

4 Heat a small pan of water with a dribble of white wine vinegar. When it starts to simmer, break in the eggs and poach gently for 2 minutes or until cooked but with a runny yolk. Remove with a slotted spoon and set aside.

5 Pour the bacon with all the juices into the salad leaves. The heat will start to wilt the leaves. Toss in the croutons and the rest of the olive oil. Season to taste and pile on 2 plates. Place a poached egg on top of each one and sprinkle with a few chopped chives.

Henry's tip: The vinegar in the water helps to strengthen the protein in the egg white. If the eggs are not super fresh, the whites can end up trailing into the water. The vinegar helps to keep them in a nice tight shape.

CUCUMBER SOUP AND SALMON TARTARE

··· SERVES 4 ···

During the Queen's Diamond Jubilee we took inspiration from the idea of a garden party to create this delicious, refreshing, gazpacho-style cucumber soup. The salmon tartare takes it from garden party to royal garden party.

FOR THE SOUP:

2 large cucumbers, peeled

400ml vegetable stock (see below)

100g crème fraîche

a pinch of salt

a squeeze of lemon

FOR THE VEGETABLE STOCK:

2 carrots, roughly chopped

1 onion, peeled and roughly chopped

2 garlic cloves, peeled

handful of parsley stalks and thyme sprigs

1 bay leaf

half a squeezed lemon

FOR THE TARTARE:

200g fillet of wild or organic farmed salmon

1 shallot, finely diced

1 tsp finely diced gherkin

1 tsp capers, finely chopped

pinch of dill, chopped

salt and pepper

a squeeze of lemon

TO FINISH OFF:

1 cucumber, peeled

sprigs of dill

good white bread and salty butter

1 For the stock, put all the ingredients in a saucepan, add water to cover, bring to the boil then simmer for 15 minutes. Turn the heat off, put the lid on and leave to infuse for 30 minutes. Strain, then measure out 400ml. (Cool and freeze the rest.)

2 Put the cucumbers and stock into a blender and blitz. Pour into a bowl and leave in the fridge for several hours to get to know each other. Remove and pour through a fine sieve to leave a clear greenish liquid. Stir through the crème fraîche. Season with salt and lemon juice. Return to the fridge.

3 For the tartare, with a sharp knife, dice the salmon up very finely and add to a bowl. Add the shallot, gherkin, capers and dill, and stir through. Season with salt and pepper and a squeeze of lemon to freshen. Place in the fridge to chill.

4 To finish, peel ribbons of cucumber down to the core. Discard the core, and pile the cucumber ribbons into 4 shallow bowls. Cup a quarter of the salmon between two tablespoons, pressing it so it holds its shape, and place in the centre. Pick some dill and scatter around the plate. Put the cucumber soup into a serving jug and pour some around the bowls at the table. Serve with a few slices of buttered bread.

PICNIC

4

HENRY

People think of a picnic as something you do on a hot sunny day, with a wicker basket and a blanket, but for me it's simply food on the hoof. Even if it's about driving somewhere and pulling into a layby to eat, that's still a picnic. The key to it all is eating sooner rather than later. Because there's nothing worse than packing up all the food and carrying it with you, and then holding out to the end of the day when everyone's grouchy and the food's gone sad and limp. Get there and eat!

TOM

Part of what it means to be British is having an uncomfortable meal somewhere in unfavourable weather conditions. But if the food is good, everything else will be all right.

THE DEVON EGG

WHEATEN BREAD

TEA-SMOKED TROUT PÂTÉ

MACKEREL 'SAUSAGE' ROLL

BLACK PUDDING SAUSAGE ROLL

CHORIZO SAUSAGE ROLL

RABBIT PIE

PLOUGHMAN'S PIE

CORNISH PASTY

MUSHROOM AND BREAD SOUP

TOMATO AND BREAD SALAD

YOGURT AND BREAD SALAD

THE DEVON EGG
··· MAKES 4 ···

This is our southern version of the Scotch egg, made for the people of Exmouth. It's crisp on the outside, with a herbed and Tabasco-spiked layer of salmon within, encasing a succulent, soft-boiled egg. The perfect snack for down the pub or out and about on a seaside walk.

4 free-range medium eggs	100g fresh crabmeat (white and brown)	**FOR THE COATING:**
400g skinless salmon fillets, cut into pieces	2 tbsp double cream	1 free-range egg, beaten
1 tbsp each of chopped dill, parsley and tarragon	salt and pepper	splash of milk
2 tsp Tabasco		pinch of salt
zest of 2 lemons		100g plain flour, seasoned
		150g white breadcrumbs
		1 litre oil, for deep-frying

1 Put the 4 eggs in a pan of boiling water and boil for 6 minutes. Remove, place in a bowl of cold water, then peel.

2 Meanwhile, put the salmon in a food processor and pulse briefly to a rough paste. Put in a bowl and add the herbs, Tabasco, lemon zest, crabmeat and cream, and season with salt and pepper.

3 In the palm of your hand, take a quarter of the salmon mix and flatten it. Place an egg in the middle and press the salmon mixture around it until it's completely covered. Do the same for the remaining eggs and chill in the refrigerator for 15 minutes.

4 For the coating, beat the egg in a shallow bowl with a splash of milk and a pinch of salt. Put the flour on one plate and the breadcrumbs on another. Take the eggs from the fridge. Roll each one in the flour, then dip into the bowl of egg, then roll in the breadcrumbs.

5 Heat the oil in a deep, heavy-based frying pan until a breadcrumb sizzles and turns brown when dropped into it. Alternatively, use an electric deep-fat fryer heated to 190°C. Fry the Devon eggs for 3 minutes, or until crisp and golden-brown.

6 Remove from the oil and drain on kitchen paper. Wrap them up while still warm and take them with you on a cold day.

WHEATEN BREAD
··· MAKES 1 LARGE LOAF ···

Tom: In Northern Ireland, we headlined the Castle Ward International Bread Festival on Strangford Lough, south of Belfast. It was an honour to be invited there. We wanted to demonstrate a recipe but didn't want to bore the audience – much as I'd love to do a sourdough, I can't have 800 people in sleeping bags while it rises – so we went in with our soda bread, knowing this was a high-risk strategy in the bread's home! True enough, we were the fourth people that day to demonstrate soda bread. But some great things came out of it. We showed people how to make their own butter from double cream, then used the buttermilk in the bread. The demo was a huge success. The people loved it, but they did tell us that what we'd made was, in fact, what they would call 'wheaten bread'. So this is wheaten bread, Baker Brothers style. With the trout pâté (see page 96), it's delicious.

450g strong wholemeal flour, plus extra for dusting	1 tsp bicarbonate of soda	200ml full-fat milk
1 tsp sea salt	50g oats, plus extra for the tin	200ml buttermilk
2 tsp caster sugar	20g butter, plus extra for the tin	
	100ml black treacle	

1 Heat the oven to 170°C/Gas 3. If you have one, place a baking stone in the oven to heat for 10 minutes.

2 Put the flour, salt, sugar, bicarbonate of soda and oats in a bowl, and mix to combine.

3 Gently heat the butter and treacle in a pan until melted. Add the mixture to the dry ingredients, along with the milk and buttermilk. Mix well until you reach a soft, wet dough. It will seem wet, but don't worry, it's just right, and it makes fantastic bread.

4 Grease a large (2lb) non-stick loaf tin with butter and dust with a sprinkling of oats. Place the dough in the loaf tin and sprinkle the top with a light scattering of oats. If you want a loaf that doesn't rise too much in the centre – for example, if you want an even square for making sandwiches – then gently indent the centre of the dough with wet knuckles, so it's lower than the edges. It will rise up to meet the edges as it bakes. Cover with foil. Bake in the oven, on the hot baking stone, for 35 minutes, then remove the foil and bake it for a further 10 minutes to get some colour on top. Remove from the oven and let it cool on a wire rack.

TEA-SMOKED TROUT PÂTÉ

··· SERVES 6–8 ···

Hot-smoking in your kitchen is a quick and easy thing to do. The trout cooks
while it smokes; the smoking also preserves it. If you've got good local trout you
can use – as we did in Bourton-on-the-Water – then it would simply be rude not to.
Trout has a delicate flavour, and the lightness of the tea goes very well with it.
Serve with wheaten bread (see page 93).

FOR THE HOT-SMOKED TROUT:

50g caster sugar

50g sea salt

2 whole rainbow trout,
cleaned and gutted

150g white rice

50g loose-leaf tea

50g soft brown sugar

drizzle of olive oil

FOR THE PÂTÉ:

500g hot-smoked trout, flaked,
bones and skin removed

100g crème fraîche

zest of 1 lemon, juice of half

1 tbsp grated horseradish

a good pinch of paprika

small handful of chopped herbs,
such as chives, dill and parsley

salt and pepper

KIT:

tin foil

2 similar-sized deep metal trays

a wire rack to position between
the trays

1 To smoke the trout, first mix the caster sugar and salt together. Rub all over the trout, inside the cavity and all over the skin. Set aside for 30 minutes to firm up the flesh.

2 Put tin foil in the bottom of one of the metal trays (this is to protect the tray as much as anything else). Mix the rice, tea and sugar for the smoke, and sprinkle on the foil. Put the tray on the hob and turn the heat up. Brush excess salt and sugar from the trout, lightly oil the skin so it doesn't stick, then place it skin-side down on the wire rack and balance it on top of the metal tray. As the tray heats up, the mixture will start to smoke. As soon as it does so, turn the heat down. Place the other metal tray upside down on top. It if doesn't fit well, seal the edges with tin foil.

3 Smoke the fish for 6 minutes. Turn the heat off and, keeping the lid on, allow the fish to sit until cooled: about 30 minutes.

4 To make the trout pâté, remove the skin and fillet the smoked trout, ensuring you remove all the bones. Roughly flake the flesh into a bowl.

5 In a separate bowl, combine the crème fraîche with the lemon juice and zest, horseradish, paprika and chopped herbs, and mix until you have a smooth paste. Season with salt and pepper. Carefully fold in the flaked trout. Eat with wheaten bread.

MACKEREL 'SAUSAGE' ROLL

··· MAKES 4 ···

Henry: Delicious firm fish, golden flaky pastry, tart nutty filling of gooseberries, walnuts and dill – what could be better for a seaside snack? I made these once for an early summer walk along a dramatic high coastal path. They are best eaten warm, but each to their own.

4 medium mackerel, filleted and skinned (ask your fishmonger to do this if you're not confident)

1 handful of large spinach leaves

400g ready-made puff pastry

egg wash: 1 egg beaten with a pinch of salt

FOR THE GOOSEBERRY FILLING:

20ml white wine vinegar

20g caster sugar

1 small shallot, finely chopped

100g gooseberries, topped and tailed

salt and pepper

5g dill, chopped

20g walnuts, toasted and chopped

1 The gooseberry filling is almost a quick relish. Put the vinegar and sugar in a pan, bring to the boil and add the shallot and gooseberries. Cook for 5 minutes or until the fruit is soft. Season and remove from the heat. Stir in the dill and walnuts, allow to cool, then put in the fridge to firm up.

2 Put 4 of the fillets on a tray skin-side up (or where the skin used to be) and season. Using a teaspoon, mound a line of gooseberry along the middle. Place the other side on top and carefully press the edges together. Put in the fridge to firm up.

3 Bring a small pan of water to the boil, plunge the spinach in, then take it straight out with a slotted spoon and into a bowl of cold water. Remove and gently squeeze out moisture, then open out the leaves and allow to air.

4 Wrap the mackerel fillets in the spinach leaves. Overlap the leaves if it's easier and makes a better parcel. The spinach not only holds the mackerel together and tastes good, it keeps the juices from making the pastry soggy.

5 Roll out the puff pastry to a rectangle at least twice the length of the mackerel and 4 times as wide. Cut into 4 rectangles and place the stuffed mackerel on each one. Egg wash the edges of the pastry and fold the other half over. Crimp together, brush with egg wash and put in the fridge for 30 minutes to set.

6 Heat the oven to 190°C/Gas 5. Put a baking tray in the oven to get hot. Place the sausage rolls directly on the hot tray. The heat will ensure the bases of the rolls cook – we don't want soggy bottoms. Bake for 15–20 minutes or until the pastry is golden and bubbling around the edges.

BLACK PUDDING SAUSAGE ROLL

··· MAKES 6 ···

Henry: This is all about speed. I made it for fire-fighters. This was to sustain them when they were out saving lives, or rescuing cats from trees. This one lost to Tom's Chorizo Sausage Roll.

500g good-quality pork sausage meat	a few sprigs of sage, leaves picked and chopped	salt and pepper
200g black pudding, crumbled	½ tsp ground mace	1 x 500g packet shop-bought puff pastry
a few sprigs of flat-leaf parsley, chopped	½ tsp cayenne	egg wash: 1 egg beaten with a pinch of salt
	3 tbsp English mustard	

1 Heat the oven to 190°C/Gas 5. In a large bowl mix the pork, black pudding, parsley, sage, mace, cayenne pepper and mustard, seasoning with a good pinch of salt and black pepper. Mix well and squidge together.

2 Roll the block of pastry out into a large rectangle 40 x 30cm. Put the filling down the middle in a neat sausage shape, and square off the edges of the pastry. Roll one side of the pastry over the meat, then pull the other side up on top. Square off the ends then turn the roll over so the fold is underneath.

3 Divide into 6 individual sausage rolls and place on a baking sheet. Slash the top of each roll a few times, brush with egg wash and bake for 30 minutes until golden brown.

Henry's tip: If you prefer the classic sausage roll, replace the black pudding with an extra 200g pork sausage meat and make it in exactly the same way.

CHORIZO SAUSAGE ROLL
··· MAKES 6 ···

Tom: A pie for busy firefighters needs to be portable and firm, something that holds together well. I wanted it to be fire-engine red, so I gave it a paprika topping. The crimping down the side is meant to be reminiscent of a fireman's ladder. The roll was delicious. It has the pepperiness of the chorizo, and the sharpness of the lemon. A real pie-war winner.

olive oil

1 large red onion, finely chopped

1 red chilli, finely chopped

2 cloves garlic, finely chopped

2 tbsp sherry vinegar

6 raw chorizo sausages, skinned and crumbled

1 x 200g jar roasted red peppers or piquillo peppers, chopped

small bunch flat-leaf parsley, leaves picked and roughly chopped

zest of 1 lime

zest and juice of 1 lemon

1 egg yolk

salt and pepper

1 x 500g pack of shop-bought puff pastry

egg wash: 1 egg beaten with a pinch of salt

pinch of smoked paprika

1 Heat the oven to 200°C/Gas 6. Heat a little olive oil in a pan on a medium heat, add the red onion and chilli and cook for 5 minutes until beginning to soften and turn sweet. Add the garlic and sherry vinegar and cook until the liquid has almost disappeared. Add the crumbled chorizo and cook for 5 minutes until a little of the oil has been released.

2 Drain off the excess oil and put the mixture into a bowl to cool down. Once cool, add the peppers, parsley, lime and lemon zest and lemon juice. Stir in the egg yolk and mix well, then season with salt and pepper if needed.

3 Roll the pastry out into a large sheet about 50 x 40cm. Cut along the middle down the length of the pastry so you have 2 long strips. Spoon half of the filling along the centre of one of the sheets, and use a brush to egg wash one long side of the pastry. Roll the other side of the pastry over the filling and seal this flat side with a fork. Do the same with the other strip. Trim off the ends to neaten, then cut each sausage into 3.

4 Put the sausage rolls on a baking sheet, brush all over with egg wash, then sprinkle over a little smoked paprika. Bake for 25–30 minutes until golden brown.

RABBIT PIE
··· MAKES 6 ···

Henry: This gorgeous Dick Whittington-style 'money pouch' of rabbity deliciousness spiked with tarragon is perfect for hungry farmers on the move, and it beat Tom's Ploughman's Pie in the food-for-farmers pie-off. A cold day in the field – what better than a nice bit of rabbit? It might also qualify as revenge for farmers.

500g rabbit, diced

2 tbsp oil

knob of butter

100g bacon lardons

2 onions, diced

2 cloves garlic, chopped

good pinch of fresh thyme

salt and pepper

100g wild mushrooms, sliced

1 carrot, finely diced

1 potato, finely diced

1 tbsp plain flour

400ml chicken stock

splash of sherry vinegar

small handful tarragon, finely chopped

6 sprigs of rosemary and 6 short pieces of string to 'tie' up the pies (optional)

egg wash: 1 egg beaten with a pinch of salt

FOR THE SHORTCRUST PASTRY:

600g strong white flour

150g cold beef dripping, broken into pieces

150g cold butter, diced

2 tbsp ice cold water

1 First make the pastry. In a food processor, blitz the flour and fats together, or rub the fats into the flour by hand. Add the iced water and knead until it just comes together. Wrap tightly in clingfilm and chill in the fridge for at least 30 minutes.

2 Quickly fry the rabbit in the oil in a hot frying pan until brown and sealed all over. Set to one side.

3 Melt the knob of butter in a large saucepan and gently fry the lardons and onions until golden-brown. Add the garlic and thyme, and season with a good pinch of salt and pepper. Stir briefly, then add the mushrooms, carrot and potato. Sprinkle the flour over and stir for 1–2 minutes. Slowly pour in the chicken stock and the sherry vinegar, stirring.

4 Put the rabbit back in, cover and simmer for 1 hour, until the rabbit is tender and the sauce is thick. Stir in the tarragon and set the mixture aside to cool down. Once cool, chill in the fridge until required.

5 Heat the oven to 200°C/gas mark 6. Divide the chilled dough into 6 balls and roll each piece out to a disc the thickness of a pound coin. Keep the shape as round as you can. Divide the rabbit mixture into 6 equal portions. Spoon the filling into the centre of each disc, then gather up the pastry around it to make a pouch. Pinch the top to seal. If you like, use string to tie a sprig of rosemary round the top of each pie. When all the pies are done, place on a baking sheet, brush with egg wash and bake for 35 minutes until golden.

PLOUGHMAN'S PIE

··· MAKES 6 ···

Tom: This was Henry's and my first pie war, and I knew Henry would do meat in his pie. I decided I wouldn't take him on head-to-head with another meat dish but instead that I'd do a portable version of the classic ploughman's dish. And all the farmers liked it – but just not quite as much as they liked Henry's! It's got strong Cheddar, and pickled onions I fried off and added chilli to, and potatoes for bulk.

		FOR THE SHORTCRUST PASTRY:
400g potatoes	200g mature Cheddar, grated	600g strong white flour
150g pickled onions	100g mixed fruit or apple chutney	150g cold beef dripping, broken into pieces
½ dried chilli, broken up	10g curly parsley, chopped	
knob of butter	smoked sea salt	150g cold butter, diced
2 tbsp olive oil	egg wash: 1 egg beaten with a pinch of salt	2 tbsp ice cold water
salt and pepper		

1 First make the pastry. In a food processor, blitz the flour and fats together, or rub the fats into the flour by hand. Add the iced water and knead until it just comes together. Wrap tightly in clingfilm and chill in the fridge for at least 30 minutes.

2 Boil the potatoes for 8–10 minutes until almost tender. Drain, cool, then chop into bite-size chunks.

3 Slice and fry the pickled onions and chilli in a bit of butter and olive oil until soft and brown. Season with some salt and pepper.

4 Mix the potatoes, hot pickled onions, cheese, chutney and parsley together in a bowl. Add a big pinch of smoked sea salt and a generous grinding of pepper.

5 Heat the oven to 220°C/Gas 7. Divide the chilled dough into 6 balls and roll each piece out to a disc the thickness of a pound coin. Keep the edges as round as you can. Divide the filling into 6 equal portions. Put filling on one half of each disc and fold the other half over to make a semi-circle that encases the filling but without meeting the other edge of the pastry. Brush the exposed lower edge with water and fold it back over to make a tight seal. Crimp the edges of the fold with your fingers.

6 Place the pies on a baking sheet, brush with egg wash and sprinkle some more smoked sea salt on top. Bake for 30 minutes until golden.

CORNISH PASTY
··· MAKES 3 OR 4 ···

If you can't get to Cornwall, try our take on the Cornish pasty, the ultimate successful savoury pie. Its roots go back to tin mining, where miners took their lunch in with them, and the thick rim of the pasty was meant for holding with blackened fingers, not for eating. It's a delicious combination of simple ingredients – amazing hot, but just as good cold. More than that, the pasty is in our nation's psyche.

Tom: We have family in Cornwall we visit on holiday, so for us the pasty is family and holiday all wrapped up. You can't go down there and guarantee it's going to be sunny, but you can guarantee a nice pasty. One of my favourite things is to cycle to St Just, get to McFadden's the butcher, and have what I believe to be one of the finest pasties ever. Or you send someone else to get the pasties while everyone puts the tents up. They return with the pasties and everything comes together with a thermos of tea. That means holiday to me.

100g diced potato	Worcestershire sauce	**FOR THE SHORTCRUST PASTRY:**
salt and pepper	1 tbsp butter	300g strong white flour
100g diced swede	egg wash: 1 egg beaten with a pinch of salt	150g cold beef dripping, broken into pieces
50g diced onion		
100g diced hanger or skirt steak		2 tbsp ice cold water

1 First make the pastry. In a food processor, blitz the flour and fat together, or rub the fat into the flour by hand. Add the iced water and knead until it just comes together. Wrap tightly in clingfilm and chill in the fridge for at least 30 minutes.

2 Heat the oven to 170°C/Gas 3. Divide the pastry into 4 equal balls and roll them out into discs about 3mm thick. They should be a good 20cm across.

3 Divide the potato between the discs, putting it in the middle, and season with salt and pepper. Next comes a layer of swede, then onion. Season again. Top with a scatter of diced beef. Splash with a little Worcestershire sauce and dot with the butter.

4 Fold the pastry over and crimp the edges into a pasty shape. Brush with egg wash and bake for 40 minutes until golden brown and cooked. Eat while still warm, or when cold.

MUSHROOM AND BREAD SOUP

··· SERVES 4–6 ···

Tom: This is a great way to use up bread. Last winter our kitchen was turned into a soup kitchen as my wife Anna, sometimes assisted by me, created soups for our four shops. It required some powerful kit, such as a bazooka-type blender that you hold up over your shoulder. The mushroom soup was delicious, and we happened at the time to have a Sherston loaf too many – as bakers we seem to have either too much bread at home or none at all – so I suggested chucking the loaf in to thicken the soup and whizzing it up with the massive blender. It was great. Anna now makes this on a domestic scale for us to eat as a family. The bread gives the soup a lovely texture. In the world of soup, it's quite different. It also satisfies my wife's addiction to mushrooms, an addiction that's been passed on to our three-year-old daughter. It's very good to take with you in a thermos on an autumnal outing.

200g good bread that needs using up	1 onion, chopped	2 leeks, chopped
500ml milk	1 tsp salt	1kg mushrooms, chopped or torn into pieces
1 tbsp olive oil	2 garlic cloves, chopped (optional)	500ml water
knob of butter	2 sprigs of thyme, leaves picked (optional)	black pepper

1 Break the bread into the milk and leave it to soak.

2 Heat the oil and butter in a saucepan over a medium heat, then add the onions and salt, and fry for 3–5 minutes until softened. Add the garlic and thyme, if using, and fry for another 1–2 minutes.

3 Add the leeks and mushrooms, stir well, and cook until the mushrooms start to soften and release their liquid. Then add the soaked bread and its milk, and the water. Bring almost to the boil, cover and simmer for 10 minutes.

4 Remove from the heat. Allow to cool a little, then blend with a hand-held blender or in a liquidizer, adding more water if necessary to reach the desired consistency. Season with pepper, and extra salt if required.

TOMATO AND BREAD SALAD

··· SERVES 3–4 ···

Tom: If you make your own bread and it dries out, you really don't want to throw it away, so this is one of the great things you can do with it. And how good it is: the combination of vinegar, oil, fresh herbs and tomatoes with the juice-soaked bread is delicious. It's a very portable salad, great for picnics – like the Yogurt and Bread Salad on the facing page.

pinch of salt	10 black olives, pitted	50ml extra virgin olive oil
3 thick slices of stale sourdough	1 tsp fine capers	black pepper
4 vine ripe tomatoes	small bunch of fresh basil	
1 red onion	15ml red wine vinegar	

1 Fill a bowl with cold water and sprinkle in some salt. Cut the crusts off the bread and tear into smallish chunks. Plunge the bread into the water and remove after 5 seconds. Squeeze out the excess water and place in a salad bowl.

2 Chop the tomatoes into irregular pieces and add to the salad bowl. Some remove the skin and seeds but I find the skin inoffensive when fresh, and the seeds have more flavour than the flesh.

3 Slice the red onion very thinly and add with the olives and capers to the dish. Rip up the basil and add that too.

4 Whisk up the vinegar and olive oil, add a little salt and a generous amount of black pepper. Toss into the salad bowl and mix. The salad should look positively rustic and messy. Leave for at least 30 minutes so the vinegar and oil can do their magic. Eat outside at ambient temperature.

Tom's tip: Made well this is heaven, made badly and it's average. Having all the ingredients at room temperature (or outside on a warm day) and of the finest quality is a must.

294616

YOGURT AND BREAD SALAD

··· SERVES 4 ···

This salad is another delicious way to use up hand-made bread that's going dry. It's even better the day after being made. A very healthy, no-cooking supper, which is perfect if you've indulged too much recently. It also makes very good picnic food.

200g stale white bread (sourdough is best)	2 tomatoes	juice of 1 lemon
	½ red onion	75g pitted black olives
200g live yogurt	6 spring onions, white parts only	3 heaped tsp za'atar
100ml milk	½ cucumber	2 pinches of sea salt
25g flat-leaf parsley, leaves picked	1 red chilli	sumac, to serve (optional)
	1 sweet red pepper	

1 Soak the bread in a bowl with the yogurt and milk. Finely chop the parsley, tomatoes, red onion and spring onion and add to the bowl.

2 Halve the cucumber lengthways (don't bother peeling it unless you want to), deseed with a teaspoon, and slice it; add it to the bowl.

3 Halve and seed the chilli and the red pepper, then slice them and add them to the bowl along with the lemon juice, olives, za'atar and sea salt. Mix together and set aside for the flavours to get to know one another. Sprinkle with sumac to serve, if you like.

Tom's tip: Lots of other garden produce and salad ingredients work well in this salad. Experiment as much as you like.

AFTERNOON TEA

TOM

If you've been working hard, and you take just a little time for the ritual of tea and some home-made cake, you can gather your thoughts, get yourself centred, then power through what's left of the day. It's also something for the kids when they come home from school.

HENRY

Everyone has a mid-afternoon lull; it's universal. These times of day for food are really important. If you just keep going, you'll wind down. This is our most feminine chapter, and it's introduced by our tea expert, Kate of Lahloo Teas in Bristol.

··········· ✤ ···········

THE MAGIC OF TEA

SWEET CHERRY MERINGUE PIES

PASSION FRUIT TARTS

TOM'S SCONES

BOURBONS

CUSTARD CREAMS

JAMMIES

BATTENBURG

PEAR LOVELIES

BLACKPOOL PLEASURE CAKE

CHERRY JUBILEE TARTS

CHESTNUT QUEENIES

FRUIT FLAPJACKS

SASHA'S CHOCOLATE CAKE

HIKER BARS

THE MAGIC OF TEA

By Kate Gover of Lahloo Tea

There's nothing more comforting than making tea, an ancient, simple, everyday ritual that takes place in households all over the world. In Britain, there's nothing we like more than putting the kettle on, arranging our favourite cups and enjoying a good cuppa. Tea gets us through the day. It restores, calms and refreshes us at any time, but especially in the mid-afternoon. You can drink it alone, or with friends and family. It is the drink that fuels Britain.

Maybe it's because of our climate. Tea is just what you need on a cold rainy day when you are sitting by the fire with hot buttered crumpets and a good book. Maybe it's because of tea's many acclaimed qualities. Whatever the reasons, since the famous nineteenth-century tea clippers such as *Lahloo* and *Cutty Sark* first raced back to the UK with their prized cargoes, Britain has adopted tea as its national drink. And thanks to the resurgence of beautiful independent tea shops, like Bristol's Lahloo Pantry and London's Postcard Teas, not really seen since the 1920s, we are more adventurous than ever with our tea.

We are exploring a whole world of tea, which we seemed to have forgotten, thanks to the terrible quality of post-war British tea – not so much leaves as dust – which got us hooked on milk and sugar. We are discovering that the leaves our great-grandparents used to enjoy are really very good. The myths surrounding tea are being broken down and we are learning more about tea's provenance, qualities and flavours. But do you know your oolong from your Assam?

Amazingly, all the different kinds of tea – white, green, oolong, black and pu'erh – come from the same plant, *Camellia sinensis*. And like wine, coffee and chocolate, a tea's unique characteristics are influenced by its 'terroir' – where it's from, what the soil is like, how high the land is and what the weather conditions are, not to mention who produced it and the traditions and rules they observe. There's so much more to tea than that sad little bag . . .

Go on, ditch the teabags. Most are made with inferior leaves, or dust (little better than the factory floor sweepings), and most companies use chlorine-bleached paper that impairs the flavour. Treat yourself to a proper teapot. To keep your leaves fresh, and to protect them from air and moisture, store them in pretty tea caddies. Be patient when making tea. It may take a little bit longer for the leaves to release their flavours, but it's worth the wait.

Once you've bought yourself beautiful tea, make sure you use the right water. First, if the water where you live is hard or very chlorinated, use a filter jug or bottled mineral water. Secondly, getting the right temperature is vital: use freshly boiled water cooled for 30 seconds for black tea, 1 minute for oolong and white tea, and 2 minutes for green tea.

CHOOSING
THE TEA

If you like your tea fortifying in the morning with your toast or bacon sarnie and you do love a splash of milk, choose a hearty black tea. Indian Assam and Kenyan teas really hit the spot. If you like tea without milk and like it to pack a smoky punch with brunch, go for something like a Sri Lankan cinnamon-smoked tea, a Japanese black tea, or a Taiwanese charcoal-roasted oolong.

For an invigorating breakfast tea with a difference, try a Japanese steamed green tea, such as sencha, or popped rice green tea, genmaicha. Or maybe try 'mighty matcha', a fine-milled, bittersweet green tea with more than a hundred times the antioxidants of loose-leaf green tea, plus vitamins and minerals. Matcha is the go-to tea for a real kick-start to the day. At the other end of the day, especially a long and hard-working one, white and jasmine teas from China are wonderfully soothing and rejuvenating.

Arguably most important of all is the tea for an afternoon pick-me-up, which is what this chapter is all about. Try one of the revitalizing, crisp Chinese green teas. For something more rich and floral, go for a light oolong. For a delicate but feel-good antioxidant boost, try a white tea. Earl Grey, a citrusy, real bergamot-infused black tea that is quintessentially British, is – it goes almost without saying – the classic partner to afternoon treats. If you're feeling indulgent, try the 'champagne of tea', Darjeeling Second Flush, a deliciously fragrant black tea. Or for something a little richer, try an autumn-picked Indian black tea, or a juicy, sweet Kenyan black tea, or a rich, fragrant oolong from China.

Take a little time to discover the wonderful world of tea.

Kate Gover

www.lahlootea.co.uk
www.lahloopantry.co.uk

SWEET CHERRY MERINGUE PIES

··· MAKES 6 ···

Tom: For this pie competition, Henry and I were making pies for trainee hairdressers, and I felt that, more than any of my other pies, how this looked mattered. Lemon meringue was the starting point. I swopped the lemon for cherry, and I created a coiffured meringue topping with red raspberries running over it like highlights. Then I added crushed pistachios to bejewel it. It looked impressive, and they loved it almost as much as Henry's, but not quite as much. I think the reason Henry's Passion Fruit Tart (see overleaf) won was that the word 'passion' resonated with them. That seemed to swing it for him. These are still crackin' and beautiful pies though.

225g plain flour, plus extra for dusting	**FOR THE CHERRY FILLING:**	**FOR FINISHING:**
100g icing sugar	2 x 400g cans cherries in juice, drained	handful of raspberries, mashed
110g cold butter, cubed	juice and zest of 1 lime	handful of pistachios, roughly crushed
4 egg yolks	1 heaped tbsp sugar	**KIT:**
pinch of salt	good swig of Amaretto	6 x 12cm tart tins
splash of milk	**FOR THE MERINGUE TOPPING:**	baking paper and baking beans or dried rice
1 vanilla pod, split and seeds scraped out	6 egg whites	
	400g golden caster sugar	

1 To make the sweet pastry, rub together the flour, icing sugar and cold butter until it resembles fine breadcrumbs. Then add the egg yolks, salt, milk and vanilla seeds. Mix until it comes together into a dough, then wrap in cling film and chill for 30 minutes.

2 Put all the filling ingredients in a saucepan and simmer gently for 15 minutes until sticky and jammy.

3 Divide the pastry into 6 equal pieces. On a lightly floured surface, roll each piece out to pound-coin thickness and about 2cm bigger than the individual tart tins. Lift the pastry into each tin, press it gently into the base and sides. Line with baking paper and fill with baking beans or dried rice. Chill for 10 minutes.

4 Heat the oven to 200°C/Gas 6. Blind-bake the pastry cases for 6 minutes, then pull the paper and baking beans out and put the cases back in the oven for 5 minutes until cooked through. Trim off the excess pastry with a knife to leave a neat edge. Turn the oven down to 110°C/Gas ¼.

5 To make the meringue, put the egg whites and sugar in a heatproof bowl set in a pan of boiling water for a couple of minutes until the sugar has dissolved. Then pour the mixture quickly into a stand-up mixer and whisk on high for 8–12 minutes until glossy and fluffy and when you pinch with your finger all the sugar grains are gone. If you don't have a stand-up mixer, hand-held electric beaters will do. It's not an option to do this by hand, however.

6 Now assemble the tarts. Place a heaped tablespoon of the cherry mixture into each tart shell and top with about 4 tablespoons of meringue. Use a teaspoon to drizzle over some crushed raspberries and sprinkle over the pistachios.

7 Bake in the very low oven for 45 minutes until the meringue is set. Serve them warm or cold.

Tom's tip: For chewy meringue middles, turn the oven off and leave the pies in there overnight.

PASSION FRUIT TARTS

··· MAKES 6 ···

Henry: I decided to woo the trainee hairdressers with passion fruit, which everybody loves. Plus I don't know any girl who doesn't like crème brûlée – the crunch, the custard – and here it is in a portable tart. And it might not look like a lot, but once you bite into it, you've got the cream, the tart passion fruit and a nice buttery pastry, and it's a winner.

FOR THE PASTRY:

225g plain flour

100g icing sugar

110g cold butter, cubed

4 egg yolks

pinch of salt

splash of milk

1 vanilla pod, split and seeds scraped out

FOR THE CUSTARD:

600ml double cream

6 egg yolks

2 tbsp golden caster sugar

2 tbsp cornflour

1 vanilla pod, split and seeds scraped out

TO FINISH THE TARTS:

1 egg, beaten, to glaze

6 passion fruit, halved

6 tsp caster sugar

KIT:

a 6-hole cupcake tray

baking paper and baking beans or dried rice

blowtorch, for caramelizing

1 To make the pastry, rub together the flour, icing sugar and cold butter until it resembles fine breadcrumbs. Add the egg yolks, salt, milk and vanilla seeds and bring together into a dough. Wrap in cling film and chill for 30 minutes.

2 On a lightly floured surface, roll out the pastry to the thickness of a pound coin. Use a 10cm pastry cutter to cut out 6 circles. Gently tease the pastry circles into the cupcake holes and press right down to the edges; don't worry if they fold and overlap a little at the top. Line each case with baking paper and fill with rice or baking beans. Chill for 10 minutes.

3 Heat the oven to 200°C/Gas 6. Blind-bake the tart cases for 8 minutes, then remove the paper and beans and bake for another 2 minutes until cooked through. Leave to cool.

4 To make the custard, gently heat the cream in a saucepan. Whisk the eggs, sugar, cornflour and vanilla seeds in a bowl. Once the cream is warm, pour it over this mixture, whisking as you go. Then transfer the whole lot into a pan and cook on a very low heat for about 15 minutes, whisking all the time until it is as thick as tinned custard.

5 Lightly brush the tart cases with beaten egg. Scoop the seeds from each passion fruit into the bottom of each tart. Top up with the custard and put in the fridge for at least 30 minutes for the custard to set.

6 Sprinkle the caster sugar in a thin layer over the top of the custard. Heat with a blowtorch until caramelized, then leave to set and harden before serving.

TOM'S SCONES

··· MAKES 10 ···

Tom: My uncle Sam and I went to Japan and made just shy of 15,000 scones by hand, and this is the recipe we used. You can prepare the mixture a little ahead of time, up to the point of adding the liquid. Once the baking powder gets wet, however, it starts its work and you need to move quickly to get the scones in the hot oven. For a light scone, a wetter dough is best. Don't over-handle the dough mixture or the gluten in the flour will start to make them tough.

360g plain white flour, plus extra for dusting	½ tsp salt	1 egg, beaten, to glaze
90g sugar	2 tsp baking powder	clotted cream and a red berry jam, to serve
90g unsalted butter, cubed	225ml milk	
	90g sultanas (optional)	

1 Combine the flour and sugar in a bowl. Add the butter and rub in until you have a texture like fine breadcrumbs. Add the salt and baking powder. You can prepare this far in advance.

2 When you are ready to bake the scones, heat the oven to 210°C/Gas 7. If you have a baking stone, put it in the oven now to heat up. Line a baking tray with baking paper.

3 Pour the milk into the flour and butter mixture. If you want fruited scones, now is the time to add the sultanas. With a few light turns of your hands, bring the mixture together into a dough.

4 Turn the dough out on to a floured work surface and lightly press out to about an inch (2.5cm) deep. Dust the top with flour and use a 3-inch (7.5cm) cutter to press out your scones. (With a smaller cutter, you'll get more scones. I like to use a fluted one.)

5 Place the scones on the baking tray, leaving a small space between each for them to expand. Brush the tops with a beaten egg and bake for 12–15 minutes or until the tops and bottoms are golden and the sides are still pale.

6 Split open while warm and eat with clotted cream and jam.

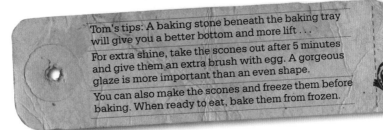

Tom's tips: A baking stone beneath the baking tray will give you a better bottom and more lift . . .

For extra shine, take the scones out after 5 minutes and give them an extra brush with egg. A gorgeous glaze is more important than an even shape.

You can also make the scones and freeze them before baking. When ready to eat, bake them from frozen.

THREE TEA-TIME
CLASSICS

Biscuits like these are so much nicer when you make them fresh
at home. When you do, all you have to think about is making them
delicious (instead of taking into consideration transport, cost
and shelf-life, like the manufactured ones). Recreating these
tea-time institutions is a lot of fun, and a great way to show off.
They will keep for a week in a tin.

BOURBONS

··· MAKES 12 ···

Rich and buttery chocolate biscuits, sandwiching sweet chocolate filling – mmm!
Irresistible. These are generously sized, and wicked with a cuppa.

FOR THE BISCUIT:

100g salted butter,
at room temperature

100g soft brown sugar

2 tbsp Golden Syrup

225g plain flour,
plus extra for dusting

30g best quality cocoa powder

1 tsp bicarbonate of soda

FOR THE FILLING:

150g icing sugar

100g butter, at room temperature

2 tbsp cocoa powder

2 tbsp cooled strong coffee

1 Heat the oven to 150°C/Gas 2.
Line a baking tray with baking
paper (you might need two).

2 Cream the butter and sugar
together until light and fluffy,
then beat in the syrup. Sift the flour,
cocoa and bicarbonate together, then
add to the butter and sugar and knead
together to create a stiff paste. Knead
the dough briefly, wrap in cling film
and let it firm up in the fridge for
20 minutes.

3 On a flour-dusted surface, roll the
paste out into an oblong about 5mm
thick and a good 36 x 30cm. Cut into
4 strips about 8cm wide and 30cm long,
then cut each strip into 6 equal-sized
fingers, so each finger will be about
5 x 8cm. (Don't make them too small or
they will be fiddly to sandwich together,
and to eat.) Place on the lined baking
tray (trays). Any offcuts can be rerolled
and baked as a treat for the chef. Bake
for 12–14 minutes until the already
dark biscuits look matt. Leave to
cool on a rack.

4 To make the filling, sift the icing
sugar into a bowl. Beat in the butter,
then add the cocoa powder, then the
coffee, and beat until smooth. Sandwich
the cooled fingers together.

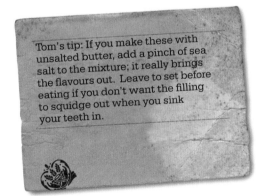

Tom's tip: If you make these with
unsalted butter, add a pinch of sea
salt to the mixture; it really brings
the flavours out. Leave to set before
eating if you don't want the filling
to squidge out when you sink
your teeth in.

CUSTARD CREAMS

··· MAKES 8 ···

Anything with custard in it is a good thing in our eyes. These delicious, buttery, custardy beauts were developed for Kate Gover and Lahloo Tea for Glastonbury Festival. They shout, 'Eat me!'

FOR THE BISCUIT:	3 tbsp custard powder	75g custard powder
100g salted butter, at room temperature	1 tsp baking powder	50g butter, at room temperature
	1 egg	1 tbsp boiling water
3 tbsp caster sugar	1 tbsp milk to bind	
175g plain flour, plus extra for dusting	**FOR THE FILLING:**	
	75g icing sugar	

1 Heat the oven to 180°C/Gas 4. Line a baking tray with baking paper.

2 Cream the butter and sugar together until light and fluffy. Sift the flour, custard powder and baking powder together, then add to the butter and sugar to create a crumbly mixture. Beat the egg and milk together, pour into the mixture and bring the ingredients together into a ball. Knead the dough briefly, wrap in cling film and let it firm up in the fridge for 20 minutes.

3 On a flour-dusted surface, roll the paste out into a long strip about 5mm thick and a good 16 x 40cm. Cut into 2 long strips of 8 x 40cm, then cut each strip into 8 fingers about 5cm wide. You should end up with 16 fingers of more or less 5 x 8cm. Place on the lined baking tray. Bake for 15 minutes until golden, then transfer to a rack and leave to cool.

4 For the filling, sift the icing sugar and custard powder together, then beat in the butter, then add the boiling water and beat until smooth. Sandwich the cooled biscuits together.

JAMMIES

··· MAKES 8 ···

Whether stars or hearts, these windows into yummy jam are simple and beautiful.
An old Hobbs House Bakery classic, they are glorious with tea. Like the bourbons
and custard creams on the previous pages, these make generous-sized biscuits
for the big-hearted.

70g caster sugar

150g salted butter,
at room temperature

220g plain flour, plus
extra for dusting

jam of your choice and
icing sugar, to finish

1 Heat the oven to 210°C/Gas 7.
Line a baking tray with baking
paper. You need a round biscuit cutter
of 8cm, or a fine teacup. You also need
tiny shaped cutters – stars, hearts, etc.
– or a steady hand, to make the centres.

2 Beat the sugar and butter together
until fluffy, then add the flour and
mix until there are no flour lumps left.
Knead the dough briefly, wrap in cling
film and let it firm up in the fridge
for 20 minutes.

3 Roll out the pastry on a floured
work surface to about 5mm thick.
Cut out 16 rounds. Press out the centres
of 8 of the rounds. Place on the baking
tray and bake for 8–10 minutes or until
the edges just start to colour. Set aside
to cool.

4 Once they have cooled, spoon jam
into the centre of the bases – don't
spread it right to the edge or it will squirt
out when you eat – and put the cut-out
biscuits on top. Dust with icing sugar.

Tom's tip: Don't waste the cut-out
middles. Either bake them just as
they are, for a tiny sweet treat, or
put them together and reroll them
to make another jammie.

BATTENBURG

··· SERVES 8 ···

Tom: This cake reminds me of my grandfather David Herbert. In the early 1980s he got into skiing, in his sixties, and he would ski in a woollen suit with a tie on and a Union Jack bobble hat. My grandma would wear a big furry hat and put spikes on her shoes and go from café to café and drink hot chocolate. For a period, they took my brother George and me with them. And they always took a box full of home-made Battenburg. They'd make tea in their hotel bedroom – Grandma didn't trust anyone to make tea the way she liked it – and eat cake. We make this in the Hobbs House Nailsworth café. It always sells really well 'cause it tastes so good.

100g salted butter, at room temperature	½ tsp baking powder	**TO FINISH:**
100g caster sugar	ruby red colour paste (from any cake decorating shop) – supermarket red food colour will work	5 tbsp apricot jam
2 free-range eggs		1 tbsp water
50g ground rice or semolina		225g almond paste/marzipan
100g self-raising flour	a few drops of rosewater	icing sugar, for dusting

1 Heat the oven to 150°C/Gas 2. Grease and line a 6 x 8 inch Battenburg tin (available online).

2 Beat together the butter, sugar, eggs, ground rice, flour and baking powder until smooth. It's quite a dense mixture, which will make a firm cake that holds together well. Lightness and fluffiness isn't the aim with this sponge.

3 Divide about half the cake mixture between 2 sections of the Battenburg tin. I use a piping bag for neatness, but a spoon will also do. Add some red colour to the remaining cake mixture – you want it a deep pink colour – along with the rosewater, and pipe or spoon into the other 2 sections.

4 Bake for about 25 minutes or until springy to the touch. Turn out on to a wire rack and cool. Trim the edges.

5 Put the apricot jam and water into a pan and bring to the boil. Using a pastry brush, brush the cake strips liberally with the hot jam, then stick them together so you have a pink and white sponge at the bottom then vice versa at the top.

6 Sprinkle a sheet of greaseproof paper with icing sugar and roll out the almond paste into an oblong shape long enough and wide enough to accommodate the sponge. Brush the almond paste with jam, roughly where the sponge will go so that all sides will be covered. Put the sponge on top of the brushed jam and, using the greaseproof paper, roll the sponge up with the almond paste. The paper helps to get a nice neat finish. Trim the edges, and your beautiful Battenburg is made.

PEAR LOVELIES

··· MAKES 16 ···

Tom: Pear lovelies were created for the people of Bourton-on-the-Water, and are heavily influenced by all things Cotswolds. We bake them in tiny loaf tins, and the light muscovado sugar turns them a beautiful honey colour, the colour of the local stone, so they look like little Cotswold cottages. Pear orchards and perry are popular in this area, so it's an opportunity to use local fruit. And 'lovely' is such a Gloucestershire word. 'All right, my lovely?' If you don't want to make them in mini loaf tins, use cupcake moulds or muffin trays instead.

FOR THE CAKE:

5 ripe pears

juice of 1 lemon

200g light muscovado sugar

3 free-range eggs, beaten

175g unsalted butter, melted and cooled

250g self-raising flour

2 tsp ground ginger

FOR THE POACHED PEARS AND SYRUP:

2 pieces preserved stem ginger, chopped finely

200g local honey

500ml perry

2 whole pears, peeled

FOR THE CREAM CHEESE ICING:

200g cream cheese

100g icing sugar, sifted

2 drops vanilla extract

TO FINISH:

2 pieces preserved stem ginger, chopped finely

40g Demerara sugar

1 Heat the oven to 180°C/Gas 4. Grease 16 mini loaf tins or moulds.

2 For the cake, peel and core the pears, dice them into a bowl and squeeze the lemon juice over to stop them browning and give them a citrus hit. Add the muscovado sugar, eggs, cooled melted butter and mix together, add the dry ingredients and mix well, making sure there aren't any lumps.

3 Divide the cake mixture between the greased tins and bake for 20–25 minutes, until the cake is golden and firm to the touch and a skewer inserted comes out clean.

4 Meanwhile, put the chopped stem ginger, honey and perry into a saucepan. Add the whole peeled pears and poach for 20 minutes. Remove the pears and allow them to cool. Reduce the poaching liquor until thick and syrupy, to make the cake glaze. Once the cake is cooked and still warm, brush over the syrup. Allow to cool.

5 To make the icing, beat the cream cheese, icing sugar and vanilla extract in a bowl until smooth.

6 To assemble, thinly slice the poached pears, going around the core. Chop the stem ginger finely and toss in the Demerara sugar. Remove the cakes from the tins. Spoon a little cream cheese icing on top of each cake, before topping with a slice of pear and some of the chopped ginger.

BLACKPOOL PLEASURE CAKE

··· MAKES 1 BIG CAKE ···

Not your average, sedate afternoon-tea fare, this is the towering confection with which we won the votes of the lovely, high-energy people of Blackpool.

FOR THE RED CAKE:	300ml milk	1 tsp vanilla extract
225g unsalted butter, at room temperature	zest and juice of 1 orange	squeeze of lemon
	1 tsp good red food colouring	1 tbsp boiling water (optional)
300g caster sugar	FOR THE BUTTERCREAM ICING:	TO FINISH:
5 free-range eggs	125g unsalted butter, at room temperature	popping candy
350g self-raising flour		rock, smashed into small pieces
¼ tsp salt	300g icing sugar	100g soft light brown sugar

1 Heat the oven to 170°C/Gas 3. Grease a 22cm kugelhopf cake tin.

2 Beat the butter and sugar until light and fluffy: 4–5 minutes using an electric beater, whisk or mixer. Add the eggs and beat until combined. In another bowl sift the flour and add the salt, then add to the creamed ingredients in three stages, folding in with a large metal spoon. Stir in the milk, the zest and orange juice.

3 Divide the cake mixture into three-quarters and one-quarter. Add the red food colouring into the quarter of the mix and mix it in well. Fold this through the other mix to create a marbled effect. Scrape the mixture into the cake tin and bake for 45 minutes, until a skewer comes out clean.

4 Cool the cake in the tin for 15 minutes, then take out of the tin and leave to cool completely on a wire rack. Once cool, level off the base.

5 For the buttercream, beat the butter till light and fluffy, sift in the icing sugar, add the vanilla and lemon juice and mix together. If it's too thick, add the water and beat well.

6 Cut the cake in thirds and spread over a thick layer of buttercream on the bottom two layers. Divide the rock and popping candy between the layers. Sandwich the cake back together. Put the rest of the filling on the top of the cake and sprinkle over the brown sugar. Decorate it further with candy twizzles and floss and flashing lights, if you so desire!

CHERRY JUBILEE TARTS
··· MAKES 12 ···

Tom: I'm a huge fan of custard tarts, and custard just sings of lush Devon with its rolling pastures. So while we were in Exmouth it was a pretty small stretch to think of clotted cream, this wonderful local product that is really only ever served cold on the side, and to consider that, since it's a creamier cream than cream, how amazing would a clotted-cream custard be? So we made one, sunk cherries into it, put it in a pastry cup case and sprinkled almonds on top – and it's been a resounding success. We also took inspiration from the story that a chef of the time had created a dish for the Queen's jubilee and called it Cherries Jubilee. We're talking Victoria here, not Elizabeth. The recipe for that dish is lost in the mists of time, but this is our idea of what a Cherries Jubilee would be like today.

FOR THE CLOTTED CREAM CUSTARD:		TO ASSEMBLE THE TARTS:
1 vanilla pod, split open	50g plain flour, sifted	1 sheet of ready-made puff pastry (375g)
250ml milk	150g cherries	
200g clotted cream	1 tbsp golden caster sugar	40g golden caster sugar
4 egg yolks	1 tbsp semolina	40g flaked almonds, toasted
100g caster sugar		icing sugar, for dusting

1 To make the custard, place the vanilla pod in a saucepan with the milk and clotted cream and bring it slowly just up to the boil.

2 In a bowl, whisk the egg yolks with the sugar until doubled in volume, then gently fold in the flour.

3 Remove the vanilla pod and pour the milk on to the egg mixture, whisking all the time. Wipe the pan, then return the mixture to it and stir and stir over a low-medium heat until it comes up to a gentle boil. Continue to cook, stirring all the time, for 3–4 minutes or until it is thick. Remove the saucepan from the heat and set aside to cool. When almost cool, cover the surface of the custard with cling film and set aside to cool completely.

4 Quarter the cherries and remove the stones, and mix them together with the golden caster sugar and semolina.

5 Heat the oven to 220°C/Gas 7. Lightly grease a 12-hole muffin tin. To assemble the tarts, unroll the puff pastry and press out 12 rounds using an 8cm cutter. Place them in the muffin tins. They'll be a bit crinkly round the top, but that's fine. Put some custard filling on the base, and top with the cherries. Bake for 10 minutes.

6 Remove from the oven and sprinkle icing sugar over each tart, and then flaked almonds. Return to the oven for a further 10 minutes. Serve warm with a dusting of icing sugar.

CHESTNUT QUEENIES

··· MAKES 12 ···

The chestnut roasters of London must be among our original sellers of street food. The smell is amazing and the scene is timeless, but there are fewer and fewer of them now. We wanted to honour them with a recipe for our London visit that used chestnut flour. This also makes these biscuits gluten-free, which is a bonus. Of course, we had to feature marmalade too, in a nod to Paddington Bear, and as a reason to visit Piccadilly's famous food shop.

FOR THE BISCUITS:

100g butter, at room temperature

25g soft light brown sugar

25g Golden Syrup

pinch of sea salt

1 vanilla pod, halved and seeds removed on the tip of a knife

100g chestnut flour

1 tsp baking powder

a jar of Fortnum and Mason marmalade

an orange, some brown sugar and a little honey, to finish

FOR THE ITALIAN MERINGUE:

100g caster sugar

30g water

2 egg whites

1 Beat the butter and sugar together until light and fluffy. Add the syrup, salt, vanilla seeds, chestnut flour and baking powder, and let it come together into a paste. Briefly knead, then roll into a small log, wrap in cling film and put into the fridge to firm up for 20 minutes.

2 Heat the oven to 170°C/Gas 3. Line a baking tray with baking paper. Take the biscuit log from the fridge and slice into 12 rounds. Bake for 15 minutes. Remove and allow to cool.

3 For the meringue, combine the sugar and water in a small pan and bring to the boil, stirring continuously with a wooden spoon until the sugar dissolves. Reduce the heat to medium and brush down the sides of the pan with a clean, wet pastry brush to remove sugar crystals. Cook until syrup reaches 115°C (soft ball stage) on a thermometer (10–15 minutes).

4 Start whisking egg whites in the clean, grease-free bowl of an electric mixer until soft peaks form.

5 Meanwhile, bring the sugar syrup to 121°C (hard ball stage). Increase the speed to high and with the motor running, gradually pour the syrup into the egg whites. Beat at medium speed until cooled to room temperature and the meringue is thick and glossy (15–20 minutes). To assemble the biscuit, spoon the marmalade into the centre and, using a spoon or piping bag, cover with meringue.

6 Blowtorch the top of the meringue. Drizzle honey and brown sugar and zest some orange over the top.

FRUIT FLAPJACK

··· SERVES 8 ···

Tom: This rich, luscious flapjack is simplicity itself, a piece of cake. It's based on an old bakery recipe that used margarine and sugar. I wanted to make an organic flapjack, so I replaced these ingredients with butter and honey. The smell coming from that first bubbling batch was magical, and we've been enchanted into making them at Hobbs House ever since. The addition of fruit makes it even juicer.

200g dried fruit – apricots, prunes, dates or dried apples all work well

150g butter

150g honey

200g rolled oats

optional extras: all manner of seeds and nuts can be added

optional topping for the finished flapjack: dark chocolate, melted in a bowl over simmering water

1 Heat the oven to 210°C/Gas 7. Chop the fruit into small pieces and put it into a medium-sized saucepan with the butter and honey. Melt the butter and honey, stirring. Once it starts to bubble, add the fruit. Stir the fruit into the honey and butter, still over a low heat, for a couple of minutes, then add the oats. Mix well, so all the oats are coated.

2 Press the mixture into a small lined roasting tin or a lined 20cm round cake tin. Bake for 10 minutes or until the edges start to go golden. Cut the flapjack into segments or squares while it's still warm. Leave in the tin to cool down and firm up.

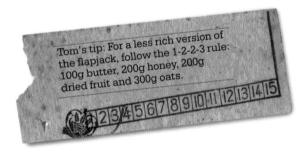

Tom's tip: For a less rich version of the flapjack, follow the 1-2-2-3 rule: 100g butter, 200g honey, 200g dried fruit and 300g oats.

131

SASHA'S CHOCOLATE CAKE

··· MAKES 1 BIG CAKE ···

Tom: This is the Bruce Bogtrotter of chocolate cakes. He's the fat kid in Roald Dahl's story *Matilda* who stole a bit of cake and then, as punishment, has to sit on the stage in front of the whole school and eat an enormous entire chocolate cake. The headmistress stands over him waiting to throw him out by the hair because she's sure he can't do it, but the schoolchildren get behind him and cheer him on to success. Sasha Jenner has been responsible for a whole delicious raft of patisserie at Hobbs House, and this has been her most popular cake.

MAKES 1 BIG CAKE		FOR THE CHOCOLATE GANACHE:
170g self-raising flour	115g caster sugar	600g plain chocolate
2 ½ tbsp good quality cocoa powder	170g Golden Syrup	600ml double cream
	140ml milk	1 tbsp Golden Syrup
1 tsp bicarbonate of soda	140ml sunflower oil	
	2 free-range eggs	

1 Heat the oven to 160°C/Gas 3. Grease and line a 20cm (8-inch) cake tin.

2 Mix the dry ingredients together. When combined, add the Golden Syrup and the milk and mix well using an electric whisk or a freestanding mixer.

3 In a jug, whisk together the sunflower oil and the eggs. Pour into the cake mix gradually, whisking after each addition. Pour into the cake tin and bake on the middle shelf of the oven for 1 hour and 20 minutes.

4 While the cake is baking, you can make the chocolate ganache. Put all the ingredients into a bowl over a pan of boiling water, stirring until the chocolate has melted. When you have a smooth glossy mixture, remove the bowl from the heat and put aside to set.

5 To check the cake is cooked, insert a skewer or knife into the centre. If it comes out clean, it's done.

6 Leave the cake in the tin for a few minutes. When slightly cool, remove from the tin and place on a wire rack to cool completely.

7 When the cake is cool and the ganache has set to a smooth spreadable texture, cut the cake in half and spread a third of the ganache over the middle of the cake. Put the top layer of the cake back on and use the rest of the ganache to cover the whole cake. To get a really smooth finish, use a palette knife dipped in a jug of boiling water. The hot knife will glide over the ganache, giving a perfect finish.

HIKER BARS

··· MAKES 12 ···

Tom: Henry and I are two of six children. Every year in the autumn half-term we would go to the Lake District for a walking holiday and relive my mum's *Swallows and Amazons* fantasies, and stay in youth hostels or old farm buildings with ice on the inside of the bathroom window. Our dad would let us have a tot of Lindisfarne mead if we were good. You could buy it from the gift shop, along with Kendal Mint Cake and Grasmere Gingerbread, which I loved. But without fail we had our hiker bars with us, which Mum always made before we went away. It keeps for weeks, and it's chewy, fruity, and the kind of thing that's robust enough that you can pack it in a biscuit tin and it rattles around in there until it's all gone. Then you get your finger in to capture all the crumbs. We now make it in our shops and it sells like hot cakes.

180g unsalted butter, at room temperature	2 medium free-range eggs	180g currants
	180g plain flour	180g sultanas
270g Demerara sugar	1 tsp baking powder	50g caster sugar

1 Heat the oven to 180°C/Gas 4. Line a baking tray about 20 x 28cm and 4cm deep with baking paper.

2 Beat the butter and sugar together until light and fluffy. This is your only opportunity to get air into this dense slab so beat the crap out of it. Break the eggs in and give the whole lot a good mix. Sift the flour and baking powder together, then add to the mixture along with the dried fruit.

3 Bake for 15 minutes, take out and press down the edges with a dough scraper or palette knife, then return to the oven for a further 10 minutes. Repeat the pressing down of the edges when you take it out of the oven if you want to get a nice even result (and so the kids can't fight over differently shaped pieces). Sprinkle with sugar. Leave to cool completely before cutting or it will fall apart.

Tom's tip: In a sealed tin, this keeps for a couple of weeks. It gets chewier, and I really like it like that.

BARBECUE

HENRY

A barbecue is all about flavour. It's a style of cooking. I would happily cook outside in the pouring rain if I had a piece of meat that would benefit from the smoky flavour barbecuing would give it, and then eat indoors. Barbecuing requires you to be active, tending, tinkering with bits of coal – it's exciting and fun. I love it.

TOM

Barbecuing is something the British have got really good at recently, and our climate lends itself to it surprisingly well, as our friend Dan Cooper, barbecue expert, explains on the next pages.

············ ❦ ············

HOW TO BARBECUE

by Dan Cooper, good friend and barbecue chef

It used to be the case that a barbecue was heralded by someone dragging a poorly constructed, grimy piece of ironwork from a cluttered garden shed on one of those rare hot and sunny British summer days. This would be followed by the cremation of sausages and burgers on an oversize blaze constructed from too many firelighters and a generous dousing of lighter fluid. But it doesn't have to be like this, and thankfully we're getting much better at barbecuing in Britain now. We have the grills, and we have the skills. We've learnt that 'barbecue' is a style of cooking, not another word for a garden party. We've learnt that our notorious damp weather need not deter us from barbecuing, but even brings us certain advantages, as you will see.

So, how to start if you are new to the game? The first requirement is good equipment. My favourite is a 57cm, good quality kettle barbecue. Barbecues have a tough life, so my advice is to buy quality, and use it more often to justify the price tag. These are perfect for all types of cooking, not just grilling and smoking, but roasting and baking too.

Fuel is the next question. The choice is between briquettes, made from coal, and lump wood charcoals (unless you are using a gas barbecue, about which more later). Good briquettes are made from highly compressed coal bound with a natural corn starch. Avoid using fuels that contain chemical accelerants and binders; these can leave unpleasant taints in the food and, although they light quickly, will also burn out quickly. Premium-brand briquettes and lump wood charcoals burn longer and better than budget brands and are worth the extra expense.

Lump wood charcoal provides fierce heat but for less time than briquettes. I use lump wood charcoal for searing and grilling robust meats such as beef, pork and lamb. Lump wood charcoal also adds a subtle smoky flavour.

For roasting and slow-cooking, always use briquettes. Made in a uniform shape, they release heat slowly and burn evenly. They offer little or no added flavour to the food; they are simply a clean-burning heat source. For really long and slow cooking, such as the succulent pulled pork on page 150, which requires 3–4 hours of roasting, or the brisket on page 172 – which requires 6 hours – choose briquettes every time.

There is only one way to light a barbecue: by using a chimney starter. You can see Henry skilfully wielding one here. This steel cylindrical device has conical wire in its base and a heatproof handle for easy pouring, and will light both briquette and charcoal quickly and efficiently, ensuring all the coals are lit to the optimum point, ready for cooking. Fill the chimney with the charcoal or briquettes, place a couple of firelighters underneath on a heatproof surface, light them up and wait for the flames to be sucked right into the centre of your stack. Coal will take about 15–20 minutes to light through. Once they are glowing on top, simply pour into your grill. I have struggled endlessly trying to light a decent fire of briquettes in the past, with the same result every time: a few in the middle are lit nicely but the ones on the outside never get a look-in. Using the chimney starter is by far the best way to do it, and brings consistency to your barbecuing.

Let's not forget gas as a cooking fuel for barbecues. There are plenty of gas grills on the market and the most important consideration is that they match the levels of temperature that charcoal can achieve. And although people might say it's not the real deal, I would argue that you still get a better flavour using a gas barbecue than cooking meat in a frying pan.

DIRECT AND INDIRECT COOKING

Whatever you're cooking, have the lid down. This helps prevent flare-ups when cooking fatty meats, and also keeps all the precious smoke flavour in with the food. Having the lid down keeps the temperature more consistent and makes the barbecue easier to control.

Direct cooking – having the food right over the heat source – is rather like grilling, and is the barbecue method most people are used to. Cooking directly is suitable for steaks, lamb chops, and other smaller pieces of meat.

Indirect cooking – having the food offset from the heat source – is more like roasting, and should be used for larger cuts of meat, pieces that take longer than 20 minutes to cook (anything up to 6 or more hours, in fact). To cook by the indirect method in a charcoal grill, you must section off the heat source. Use tongs to move the hot coals to one side to create a good-sized gap. Then position the cooking grate over the coal-free area and place your meat there. Providing you use the lid-down method, the meat will roast through evenly.

Always use briquettes for indirect, slow cooking. The very best will give you 3½ hours' cooking time. To extend the cooking time further, light up half a chimney starter full, then move the new hot coals to the barbecue using tongs.

HOLY SMOKE

For me one of the most exciting aspects of barbecuing is the smoke. I use a variety of wood chips, depending on what I'm cooking. The stronger varieties are hickory and mesquite; these exude a powerful and rich smoke that will cling to your meat. Fruit woods such as apple and cherry are a little milder, lending a more sweet and subtle flavour. There are plenty of varieties out there. I smoke my food using the indirect set-up and with the lid on. Cooking things slowly when smoking means your food has more time to absorb the smoky flavour. Meat in its raw state is most receptive to the smoke flavours.

Pre-soaking woodchips will give a longer smoke, but this is not essential. Using less is more when it comes to wood chips. If you add too many to the coals, meat can become bitter. I recommend no more than two large handfuls for one chicken. Large wood chunks can also be used, but this is for a longer, less intense smoke.

Wood-plank cooking is a fantastic way of cooking fish and other meats. The planks are pre-soaked and, although they don't give off as strong a flavour as wood chips, the steam evaporating from the wood primes the meat or fish with a wonderful nature-sweet woody flavour. See page 173 for a recipe.

We often use steam to help cook meat and keep moisture in when grilling. The beer-can chicken recipe (see page 170), for example, ensures maximum moisture content and falling-apart results. This is a really good way to get started if you want to roast whole joints of meat on the barbecue.

So, to the British climate. Our cold, thick, damp outdoor air circulating in the barbecue cook box is a bonus: it makes food deliciously juicy and moist. This is in stark contrast to an indoor fan oven, which will tend to dry meat out because it recycles hot air, which lacks moisture.

With this in mind, I think it's time, even though the sun isn't shining, to get out there, light up a chimney and have a go!

Dan Cooper

BURGER BAPS

We stuck our flag in the sand with our slider burgers and ultimate burger baps, but now we've extended the franchise. Once you've mastered the ultimate, why stop there? Here are some more burgers and baps we really like. This is a next-level series of barbecue recipes, and if you demand reward and satisfaction for your effort, then this is off the scale. If you've never baked bread before, you can tick it off the 101 things to do before you're 100. Warning: you might find it impossible to go back once you've discovered the pleasure of baking. For these baps, we've stripped back the recipe and process to the bare bones, then there are bolt-on additions that pimp the basic recipe into four delicious and distinct buns. You can cut the dough into different shapes to tell them apart if you are baking more than one variety at a time.

THE BASIC BBQ BAP

··· MAKES 8 LARGE OR 12 SMALL ···

Dusted with flour, this makes a good simple bap on its own, or add the ingredients on the following pages to make bespoke baps for your burgers.

5g dried yeast (or 10g fresh)	500g strong white flour,	10g salt
300ml tepid water	plus extra for dusting	

1 Stir the dried yeast into the tepid water and allow it to dissolve. Weigh the flour and salt into a bowl, then add the water and yeast. Mix it all together.

2 Once it has come together as a raggedy dough, turn out of the bowl and knead on a floured surface for 15 minutes until the dough is smooth, elastic and stretchy. (This takes 10 minutes in a mixer.) Place in a bowl and cover, and leave it for 30 minutes to rise.

3 Remove the dough from the bowl, place on a floured work surface and roll out until it's an inch (2.5cm) thick. Using a dough scraper or a knife, cut the dough into round shapes half the size you want your baps, then dust with flour. Place on a baking tray lined with baking paper with a gap between each one. Cover and leave for an hour in a warm place to rise.

4 Heat the oven to 230°C/Gas 8. Bake the baps for 10 minutes.

CHEESE AND ONION SEED BAPS

··· MAKES 8 LARGE OR 12 SMALL ···

These are the bespoke baps for the Pulled Pork Burgers on page 150, and will take your barbecue experience to a whole new level.

5g dried yeast (or 10g fresh)	10g salt	50g grated cheese
300ml tepid water	50g lard	
500g strong white flour, plus extra for dusting	15g black onion seeds	
	20g sugar	

1 Stir the dried yeast into the tepid water and allow it to dissolve. Weigh the flour and salt into a bowl, then add the water and yeast, the lard, onion seeds and sugar. The lard makes for a very soft dough. Mix it all together. Just when it is starting to resemble a raggedy dough, incorporate the cheese.

2 Turn out of the bowl and knead on a floured surface for 15 minutes until the dough is smooth, elastic and stretchy. (This takes 10 minutes in a mixer.) Place in a bowl and cover, and leave it for 30 minutes to rise.

3 Remove the dough from the bowl, place on a floured work surface and roll out until it's an inch (2.5cm) thick. Using a dough scraper or a knife, cut the dough into round shapes half the size you want your baps. Place on a tray lined with baking paper with a gap between each one. Cover and leave for an hour in a warm place to rise.

4 Heat the oven to 230°C/Gas 8. Bake the baps for 10 minutes.

Cheese and onion seed bap

Ras-el-hanout bap

Beetroot bap

Saffron butter bap

RAS-EL-HANOUT BAPS
··· MAKES 8 LARGE OR 12 SMALL ···

These are the bespoke baps for the Spicy Lamb Burgers on page 152. This recipe is also a nod at our country's willingness to adopt flavourings from all around the world and to turn them into something completely British. Take HP Sauce, named after the Houses of Parliament and popular for decades, yet made with tamarind and spices. Here we've borrowed the flavourings of Morocco.

5g dried yeast (or 10g fresh)	10g salt	50g black olives, chopped
300ml tepid water	50ml olive oil, plus extra for brushing	
550g strong white flour, plus extra for dusting	15g ras-el-hanout spice	

1 Stir the dried yeast into the tepid water and allow it to dissolve. Weigh 500g of the flour and the salt into a bowl, then add the olive oil, spice and black olives. Mix it all together. If the olives are very moist, you might find you need the extra 50g flour. The dough needs to be soft but not too sticky.

2 Once it has come together as a raggedy dough, turn out of the bowl and knead on a floured surface for 15 minutes until the dough is smooth, elastic and stretchy. (This takes 10 minutes in a mixer.) Place in a bowl and cover, and leave it for 30 minutes to rise.

3 Remove the dough from the bowl, place on a floured work surface and roll out until it's an inch (2.5cm) thick. Using a dough scraper or a knife, cut the dough into diamond shapes half the size you want your baps. Brush with olive oil, then place on a tray lined with baking paper with a gap between each one. Cover and leave for an hour in a warm place to rise.

4 Heat the oven to 230°C/Gas 8. Bake the baps for 10 minutes.

SAFFRON BUTTER BAPS

··· MAKES 8 LARGE OR 12 SMALL ···

Hard to imagine you can improve on the luxury of Lobster Burgers
(see page 155), but you can, with these beautiful, golden buns.

5g dried yeast (or 10g fresh)	500g strong white flour, plus extra for dusting	50g butter, at room temperature
3 strands of saffron		1 egg, beaten, plus 1 egg yolk for glaze
250ml tepid milk	10g salt	sea salt flakes

1 Stir the dried yeast and the saffron strands into the tepid milk. Allow the yeast to dissolve. Weigh the flour and salt into a bowl, then add the butter and egg. Mix it all together. The dough should be soft but not sticky. If it's too sticky, add a little extra flour.

2 Once it has come together as a raggedy dough, turn out of the bowl and knead on a floured surface for 15 minutes until the dough is smooth, elastic and stretchy. (This takes 10 minutes in a mixer.) Place in a bowl and cover, and leave it for 30 minutes to rise.

3 Remove the dough from the bowl, place on a floured work surface and roll out until it's an inch (2.5cm) thick. Using a dough scraper or a knife, cut the dough into fat rectangles half the size you want your baps, or go mad and make lobster claws: tapered finger rolls with a cut along a third of the 'claw'. Place on a tray lined with baking paper with a gap between each one, then brush with the egg yolk for a luxuriant glaze. Cover and leave for an hour in a warm place to rise.

4 Heat the oven to 230°C/Gas 8. Sprinkle the baps with sea salt flakes just before putting them in the oven to bake for 10 minutes.

Tom's tip: This makes more baps than you need for the recipe on page155; freeze the remainder, or eat them with another filling.

BEETROOT BAPS

⋯ MAKES 8 LARGE OR 12 SMALL ⋯

Gorgeous red triangles of joy to go with the Mackerel Burgers on page 154.

5g dried yeast (or 10g fresh)	10g salt	a handful of chopped fresh thyme, leaves picked
300ml tepid water	1 large or 2 small cooked vacuum-packed beetroots, blended to a fine paste	1 generous tbsp honey
500g strong white flour, plus extra for dusting		oil for brushing (optional)

1 Stir the dried yeast into the tepid water and allow it to dissolve. Weigh the flour and salt into a bowl, then add the beetroot, thyme and honey. Mix it all together. The dough needs to be soft but not too sticky.

2 Once it has come together as a raggedy dough, turn out of the bowl and knead on a floured surface for 15 minutes until the dough is smooth, elastic and stretchy. (This takes 10 minutes in a mixer.) Place in a bowl and cover, and leave it for 30 minutes to rise.

3 Remove the dough from the bowl, place on a floured work surface and roll out until it's an inch (2.5cm) thick. Using a dough scraper or a knife, cut the dough into triangles half the size you want your baps. Place on a tray lined with baking paper with a gap between each one. Cover and leave for an hour in a warm place to rise.

4 Heat the oven to 230°C/Gas 8. Bake the baps for 10 minutes. For a brilliant shine that will show off their colour, brush them with oil the moment they come out of the oven.

Tom's tips: The best kind of cooked beetroots to use for these are those that come vacuum packed in their own liquid. For an extra deeply coloured bap, use their liquid to make up the quantity of water.

This makes more baps than you need for the recipe on page 154; freeze the remainder, or eat them with another filling.

PULLED PORK BURGERS

··· MAKES 8 ···

Sticky, smoky, sweet and succulent pork, with melted cheese, fragrant green chilli mayo that kicks like a mule, and crunchy lettuce in a soft cheesy bap. What's not to love? To take the pork to the next level, throw some smoking chips on the hot coals for extra flavour.

2kg pork belly	30ml Worcester sauce	zest and juice of 1 lime
FOR THE RUB:	20g tomato purée	salt and pepper
20g sea salt (smoked if possible)	30ml cider vinegar	**TO SERVE:**
10g dark brown sugar	30g Dijon mustard	8 onion seed and cheese baps (page 143)
5g black pepper	**FOR THE CHILLI MAYO:**	
5g smoked paprika	2 egg yolks	8 slices of medium Cheddar or Swiss cheese
5g celery salt	1 tsp white wine vinegar	
5g cayenne pepper	1 tsp Dijon mustard	coleslaw (optional)
10g garlic flakes	200ml vegetable oil	1 baby gem lettuce, leaves separated
10g onion flakes	1 green chilli	

1 For the mayonnaise, whisk the egg yolks with the vinegar and mustard in a round-bottomed bowl on a folded tea towel for stability. Measure the oil into a jug, then slowly trickle it in, whisking all the time. When it's all in and you have a thick mayonnaise, chop up the green chilli as small as possible and stir it through, along with the lime zest and juice and seasoning. Keep in the fridge.

2 Mix the rub ingredients together in a bowl, then rub all over the pork belly. Leave it overnight if possible so the pork can take on all the flavours.

3 Heat the barbecue up with the charcoal on one side: we are cooking indirect here. Wrap the pork belly in a double layer of tin foil and place on the non-charcoal side. 'Low and slow' are your watchwords here. The ideal temperature is 180°C. It will take 3–4 hours for the pork to become tender. If the fire dies down, add more hot charcoal using the starter (see page 140).

4 Give the meat a probe; when it is giving and unctuous, remove it and allow it to rest, being careful not to spill any of the delicious juices from the foil. These will make your burger divine.

5 Pick the meat into a bowl in small shreds. Throw the skin and excess fat away. Mix through the juices to make the pork irresistible. Keep warm.

6 Cut the baps in half, spoon on a dollop of chilli mayo and add the pulled pork and a slice of cheese. The warmth of the pork will melt the cheese. Add coleslaw, if you feel inclined, and the lettuce. Top and give it a squash. Eat with chin-dribbling satisfaction.

SPICY LAMB BURGERS
··· MAKES 8 ···

With so many good burger recipes out there, it's nice to do one that is a little bit different. If you have made the ras-el-hanout baps (see page 145), then this really is the best filling, sweet and spicy with beautiful colours. With the weather being so dismal the summer just gone, we needed an excuse to whip up something spicy and exotic that transported us to a brighter place. Fire peppers are surprisingly fun and easy to make and taste great. They are better on the barbecue for the lovely smoky aroma, but work fine on the gas hob too.

FOR THE FIRE PEPPERS:

4 Romano peppers

1 tbsp extra virgin olive oil

1 tsp sherry vinegar

salt and pepper

FOR THE LAMB BURGERS:

1.5kg lamb mince

1 onion, diced

2 garlic cloves, chopped

1 tsp olive oil

1 tbsp each of ground cumin, coriander, cinnamon, smoked paprika and turmeric

pinch of ground cloves

1 preserved lemon, finely chopped

bunch of mint, leaves picked and chopped

salt and pepper

TO SERVE:

8 ras-el-hanout baps (page 145)

date and onion relish (facing page)

rocket leaves dressed in oil and lemon

1 First prepare the peppers. If using a barbecue, place the peppers over the heat source and cook for 10 minutes. Keep turning so they blacken on all sides. Fear not, we want it to burn. If using the gas hob, place directly on the flame and turn every so often. Don't burn your hands, use tongs. When the peppers are black and blistered all over, remove and wrap in cling film. This makes the peppers sweat and softens the flesh. After 5 minutes, remove the soggy cling film, and peel and rub the charred skin from the peppers, leaving behind the most amazing fire pepper. Cut in half and remove the seeds. Place into a bowl and toss with oil, vinegar and salt and pepper. Set to one side.

2 For the burgers, make sure to use the best quality lamb mince you can find. Heat a small pan and sweat the onion and garlic. When soft and golden, remove from the heat. In a large bowl, mix the lamb mince with the onion and garlic, the spices, preserved lemon, mint and seasoning. Give it a good mix. Divide into 8 balls and shape into burgers. Chill in the fridge for at least 30 minutes before grilling.

3 Cook the burger for 3 minutes each side on a hot grill. This gives you a nice medium burger. While the burger is cooking, split the baps and warm briefly on the grill. Spoon on some relish and some dressed rocket. Add the burger and half a fire pepper. Top, give it a squash, and in the cake hole.

DATE AND ONION RELISH

Not just good with burgers, try this with cheese on toast or any grilled meat.
The relish will keep in the fridge for a month.

20ml olive oil	1 green chilli, de-seeded and chopped	100g medjool dates, chopped
2 shallots, diced		50g sugar
1 pinch of sumac	3cm fresh root ginger, grated	75ml red wine vinegar
1 pinch of ground coriander	1 sprig of rosemary	salt and pepper
1 stick of cinnamon	200g raisins	splash of rosewater

1 In a saucepan, heat the oil and gently fry the shallots. When they start to soften, add the spices, chilli and ginger. Cook the spices for a few minutes to release their oils and aroma.

2 Add the rosemary and the dried fruit, give it a quick stir, then add the sugar and vinegar. Bring to the boil, then turn down and simmer gently for around 10–15 minutes or until the relish is thick and shiny. Check for seasoning.

3 Finish with a tiny splash of rosewater. It wants to be sweet, spicy and slightly sour. Perfect for cutting through the rich lamb.

BARBECUE

MACKEREL BURGERS

··· MAKES 4 ···

This little fishy number looks beautiful, especially in the beetroot baps.
The colours are so vivid it can't help but make people smile. Use the freshest
mackerel you can get; it makes all the difference. Mackerel, beetroot and
horseradish is a classic combo.

4 large mackerel fillets,
skinned and boned

big pinch of finely chopped parsley

big pinch of dill fronds

zest and juice of 1 lemon

1 garlic clove, crushed

salt and pepper

TO SERVE:

4 beetroot baps (page 147)

1 tsp creamed horseradish mixed
with 1 tbsp crème fraîche

small bunch of watercress,
thick stalks removed

2 pickled beetroots, sliced

1 Using a sharp knife, carefully chop the mackerel into small dice. Place in a bowl with the chopped herbs and the zest and juice of the lemon. Add the garlic and season with salt and pepper. Mix together and place in the fridge for 30 minutes while the flavours get to know each other.

2 Remove and shape into 4 burger patties about 1cm thick. Place in the fridge to firm up again.

3 Carefully fry the mackerel burgers on an oiled baking tray over the hot grill. Give them 3 minutes on each side until they are nice and golden and just cooked through.

4 Split the baps and smear with horseradish cream. Add a bundle of watercress, place the burger on top and add a few slices of pickled beetroot. Lid it and eat with a smile.

LOBSTER BURGERS
··· MAKES 4 ···

A total luxury but in the humble form of a burger, this takes a simple idea and ramps it up to make a sandwich that demands attention. If you are going to treat yourself to lobster, try to buy a native one from a decent fishmonger's. We are a country surrounded by coast so this should be possible. It will taste so much better.

2 x 700g native lobsters (get your fishmonger to kill them)	**FOR THE MARIE ROSE SAUCE:**	**TO SERVE:**
pinch of smoked paprika	4 tbsp mayonnaise (for home-made, see page 150 and leave out the chilli)	4 saffron butter baps (page 146)
1 garlic clove, crushed		1 baby gem lettuce, leaves separated
2 tbsp olive oil	1 tbsp ketchup	2 ripe vine tomatoes, sliced
juice of 1 lemon	splash of Worcestershire sauce	1 ripe avocado, peeled and sliced
salt and pepper	few drips of Tabasco (optional)	
8 rashers of smoked streaky bacon (dry cure)	small bunch of parsley or chervil, leaves picked and finely chopped	

1 First make the Marie Rose sauce. Mix all the ingredients together until you have a thick, salmon-pink sauce with green specks running through. I like mine to pack a punch but leave out the Tabasco if you prefer. Set aside. This sauce is perfect for any cocktail food action.

2 Carefully remove the lobster tail and the claw from the shell (or ask your fishmonger to do this). It's quite easy but requires a sharp knife and a small hammer. Keep the shell for stock making. Slice the tail into 1cm rings and place with the meat of the four claws in a bowl. Add the paprika, garlic, olive oil, lemon juice and seasoning. Mix together and allow to marinate for at least 30 minutes.

3 Put the slices of bacon and the lobster meat on a baking tray and place over the hot grill to cook and colour. The lobster will take about 4 minutes. If the bacon isn't crispy in this time, remove the lobster and continue with the bacon. You want it nice and crisp. Warm the baps briefly on the side of the grill.

4 Now to build the bun. Cut open the warm baps and spread with a layer of Marie Rose sauce. Place a few leaves of baby gem on, cup side up. Fill with the lobster and two slices of bacon. Top with a slice of tomato and some avocado. Lid the bun and give it that important squish before eating.

THE BEEFEATER

··· MAKES 6 ···

Tom: London has seen a revival of great hand-made burgers recently, and we wanted to give the tourists a taste of this instead of the franchised chain burgers near the tourist hotspots. This is good British beef, with the surprise of an egg inside the burger, which makes it juicy and delicious. But the killer element is the glazed crown-shaped bun. And once your jaw has dropped in pleasant surprise, it needs to drop a little further in order to fit the burger in, because it's quite a stack! We also made this in tribute to the wonderful Beefeaters at the Tower.

FOR THE CROWN BUN:

big pinch of dried yeast (or 5g fresh)

150ml tepid water

250g strong white flour, plus extra for dusting

15g lard

5g salt

egg wash: 1 egg beaten with a pinch of salt

FOR THE BURGER:

500g good quality beef mince

1 tsp smoked sea salt

1 tsp black cracked pepper

3 onions, sliced into rings and fried in a small knob of butter until soft and lightly coloured

2 tsp English mustard

2 sprigs of rosemary, finely chopped

7 medium free-range eggs

FOR THE LONDON SAUCE:

1 small bunch of flat-leaf parsley, leaves picked and finely chopped

4 tbsp mayonnaise (for home-made, see page 150 and leave out the chilli)

2 tbsp HP Sauce

½ tsp Tabasco sauce

3 gherkins, diced

zest of half a lemon

half a green chilli, finely diced

salt and pepper

TO BUILD:

2 baby gem lettuces, leaves separated

strong Cheddar cheese, thinly sliced

2 large tomatoes, sliced

1 For the crown bun, mix the yeast with the tepid water and stir until it dissolves. Weigh the flour, lard and salt into a large bowl. Add the yeast and its water. Bring together into a raggedy dough, then turn out on to a lightly floured surface and knead for 15 minutes until the dough is soft and elastic. Leave to rise for 1 hour in a covered bowl in a warm place.

2 Divide the dough into 6 and on a lightly floured surface roll into balls with your hands. Using a rolling pin, flatten them slightly. Place on baking trays lined with baking paper and brush egg wash over each bap. Cover loosely with cling film and leave in a warm place for 30 minutes.

3 Brush with a second coat of egg wash. Snip around the edge with scissors to create a crown shape. Cover loosely with cling film and leave for a final 30 minutes to rise.

4 Heat the oven to 200°C/Gas 6. Bake the baps until they are perfectly golden, about 10–15 minutes.

5 For the burgers, mix all the ingredients together in a large bowl with 1 of the 7 eggs until fully combined. Divide into 6 and shape into burger patties. Push your finger through the patties, making a hole in the middle as big as it will go before the patties start to break apart. Put on a plate and chill in the fridge for 15 minutes or until needed.

6 For the sauce, combine all the ingredients in a bowl. Adjust to your taste with salt and pepper or additional amounts of any of the other sauce ingredients.

7 Cook the burgers on an oiled baking tray on the hot grill. Fry the burgers on one side for about 4 minutes, then flip over and fry the other side. Crack one egg gently into the middle hole of each burger and fry for a further 3 minutes with the barbecue lid down so that the egg white cooks through. The burgers should be just pink and the egg yolk just runny.

8 Halve the baps and smear the bases with London sauce. Place a few overlapping leaves of baby gem and slices of tomato on top, cover with the burgers and finish off with a slice or two of Cheddar.

Tom's tips: London sauce is dangerously addictive. It's a capital condiment! Keeps for a week in the fridge.

Using egg yolk alone as the glaze for the buns will make them even more gloriously golden.

FLATBREADS

··· MAKES 6 ···

Tom: This is the perfect bread to make on a barbecue. You just heat a baking stone up on the grill, then roll the dough really thin and bake it in minutes on the searingly hot stone. You can also bake it directly on the grill. The bread doesn't puff up, like pitta, but it develops little blisters and charred spots, which are delicious. The flatbreads are great with dips and as a wrap for grilled meat. At Hobbs House one of our recent discoveries has been za'atar, a seasoning from the eastern Mediterranean, made of sumac, sesame seeds, thyme, oregano, marjoram and salt. It adds something really fresh and tasty to the bread and makes it the ideal accompaniment to meat that has been marinated or has a rub on it. We like za'atar a lot, so we've stuck our flag in it and claimed it.

5g dried yeast (or 10g fresh)	210g strong white flour, plus extra for dusting	50g sourdough (optional)
250ml tepid water, or 225ml if using the sourdough	210g wholemeal flour	40ml olive oil, plus extra for brushing
	8g sea salt	za'atar, for sprinkling

1 Dissolve the yeast in the tepid water. Combine the flours and salt together in a bowl, add the yeast and water, and sourdough if using, and give it all a good mix. As the dough comes together, turn it out on to a lightly dusted work surface and knead for 15 minutes until smooth and elastic. Put it back in the bowl, cover and rest for 45 minutes.

2 Divide the dough into 6 pieces of roughly equal size, shape them into rounds, then cover and rest them for an hour.

3 Heat the baking stone or the grill to blisteringly hot. On a floured work surface, roll the dough out as flat and as long as you can, then brush with olive oil and finish with a generous sprinkling of za'atar. Bake one at a time, on one side only, for 2 minutes at the most. If you are baking them on the barbecue, have the lid down.

HOW TO BUY
AND COOK STEAK

Henry: If I were to give you only one bit of advice about eating amazing steaks at home, it would be to go to your local butcher's and be nice to them. Build a relationship with them and they will provide you with the steaks you want. This is particularly so with the new cuts (see below) which require skilled preparation A healthy relationship will make shopping more fun and more productive.

THE FABULOUS FOUR

Fillet: The most expensive steak, loved for its soft buttery texture and its neat round shape. It comes from the inside of the lower part of the sirloin. It is a muscle that does very little, so it's very tender and has little fat. It is best served pink with a good béarnaise sauce.

Sirloin: Said to have got its name from King Henry VIII, who loved it so much he knighted it. It is, as the name suggests, the loin of the cow, similar to a pork chop. It has a mild flavour and is tender, with a covering of fat on one side. The flesh should be dense and dark with specks of marbling running through. It is best hung for a least a month to give you a really tender steak.

Rib-eye: A steak relatively new to the club, but it has certainly made its mark. Cut from the centre of the forerib, it is a steak of real flavour. When it has been

hung on the bone for a good month, to allow the muscles to break down and concentrate in flavour, it gives you the most amazingly flavoursome and tender steak. The rib-eye has quite a lot of fat, so it's very juicy and perfect for cooking over flames.

Rump, D cut: An old-school butcher's classic. A huge steak cut right across the rump, a.k.a. the cow's backside. Well hung and cut thick, grilled and served with a slick of mustard, this is a real man's steak. The rump is full of flavour, and as long as it's hung properly on the bone it can be quite tender. Compared to fillet it will require a little chewing, but what else are jaws made for?

NEW STEAKS ON THE BLOCK

Often cheaper and more flavoursome, these steaks are making a big noise. As long as they are cooked and carved right, they can be mind-blowing for a fraction of the price of the Big Four.

Unlike the Big Four, these steaks come about from seam butchery, where rather than cutting straight across the meat, you cut along the seams, so each steak is one muscle rather than several joined together. What it means is that classically cheaper cuts used mainly for stewing or mincing can be eaten as a steak with full flavour and tenderness.

The Fabulous Four

Sirloin

Rib-eye

D-cut rump

Fillet

Mouse-in-the-hole

Bistro rump

Hanger

False fillet

Pichana

Skirt steak

Flat iron

Skirt/bavette: A French bistro cut, from the flank of the cow. With its long muscle strands and open texture, it is the perfect steak for a sandwich or to have with chips. As long as the skirt is cooked pink and sliced against the grain, it will be delicious and tender. If you overcook and cut with the grain, it will be tough, chewy and dry.

False fillet: Taken from the front half of the cow just behind the blade bone, this muscle looks similar to the fillet steak, and in days gone by naughty butchers would sell it as fillet to unsuspecting customers. Thankfully those days are gone. The false fillet, if cut thinly and cooked pink, will be surprisingly tender and has a great flavour.

Flat iron: An American cut, this comes from the other side of the blade bone. When the butcher has removed the thick tendon from the middle, you are left with two long, flat muscles that have great marbling. Cooked on a hot grill after a marinade or rub, rested and sliced thin, the flat iron has an amazing flavour that will impress the biggest steak lovers.

Hanger/onglet steak: My best find. It hangs on the inside of the diaphragm, hence the name; it is classified as offal but don't be put off by this. Hanger steak is similar to skirt steak but has a much beefier flavour and is beautifully marbled. When cooked pink and sliced thin against the grain, you have the most delicious, unctuous, tender steak.

Pichana: The cap of the rump. The rump is made up of four main muscles that are best cooked separately rather than in one long slice. The pichana, a south American name, is the juicy top flap of the rump. With a nice covering of fat, it is everything that a sirloin is not. Dense and beefy, this steak is perfect for the grill.

Bistro rump: This is taken from the centre muscle of the rump steak. This is a poor man's fillet with its lean round shape, but with a far superior flavour and a cheaper price tag, it fills its boots with pride.

Mouse-in-the-hole: My favourite name. This is the top part of the shin, taken off the silverside, which is the thigh muscle. It has thick tendons running through, but when these have been seamed out you are left with beautiful steaks.

HOW TO COOK STEAK

Following a few rules will ensure excellent eating enjoyment. First, buy well. A cheap, gristly steak will never give you that much enjoyment, so buy the best you can, ideally from a reputable butcher's which sources locally and hangs the meat on the bone for at least three weeks.

If you like your meat pink, it is better to get a thick steak rather than a very thin one, as by the time it has coloured it will be cooked through.

Steak needs a hot pan like ducks need water. If you don't like your house full of smoke, don't cook steak inside. There is nothing worse than putting a steak into a cold or warm pan and letting it stew in its own juices until it turns into a piece of grey, boiled leather. Heat the pan up until it is smoking. Season the steak liberally with salt, pepper, rubs and so on, then oil the pan and put the steak in. It should sizzle! Leave it alone. Don't be tempted to shake the pan around or flip the steak. All this is doing is cooling the pan down. We want that lovely caramelization that gives us a beautiful flavour-crust. After about 2–3 minutes, turn the steak over and cook it in the same way on the other side. When cooked to your desired doneness, throw in a knob of butter and spoon it over the steak. This will give it a lovely rich shine and finish it off perfectly. Remove from the pan and let it rest.

Cooking a steak on the barbecue is not so different, except that you have less control of the heat, but you do gain so much more in flavour. The barbecue needs to be ramped up to the max – we are talking smokin'. Season the steak and cook as usual. It will take a little longer to brown on the first side, and when you turn it, it might flare up as the rendered fat drips on to the hot coals. If it does, just move the steak to a cooler part of the barbecue until the flames have subsided. When the steak is cooked, rest it as normal. Try adding a few wood chips as you cook for a more intense, smoky flavour.

HOW TO KNOW WHEN THE STEAK IS DONE

To know when steak is cooked to your liking takes a little practice. Here are a few tips to help you. A temperature probe is the most accurate (see temperatures below), but a finger-thumb test can be the next best thing. Place your thumb on each finger in turn. By prodding the fleshy drumstick of the thumb with your other hand, you'll notice it changes in firmness. As you move through the fingers, it gets firmer. This is similar to the doneness of your steak.

Index finger to thumb = rare (50°C)
Middle finger to thumb = medium rare (56°C)
Ring finger to thumb = medium (62°C)
Little finger to thumb = well done (70°C)

Chefs are always going on about resting meat – but why? Picture this. You are thrown into a boiling pot of water. What do you do? You tighten up. Your muscles would be tough and chewy. Now take yourself to a warm spa and play some soothing music. Now you are relaxed and supple – in steak terms, much tastier. If you take meat out of a frying pan and eat it straight away, it will be chewy and the juices will flow out. Leave it to rest and the muscle will relax and become tender. The juices will stay in the meat, making for better eating. So it is important always to rest meat. For steaks, the resting time is 5 minutes.

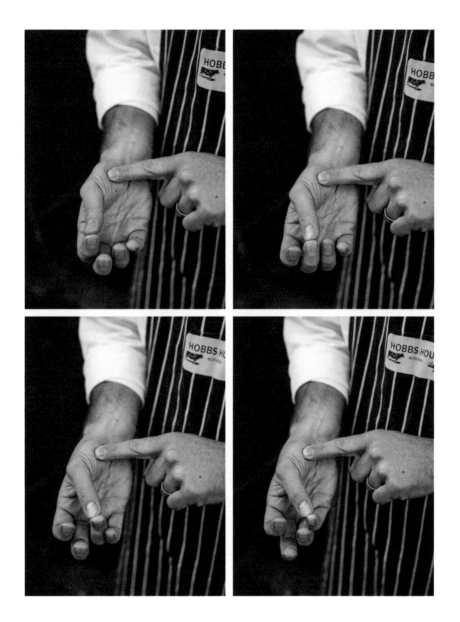

CHICKEN BEER BUTT
··· SERVES 4 ···

This backyard way to cook a chicken is also delicious and tasty and gives you a good excuse to crack open a six-pack of beer. As the chicken cooks on the barbecue, the beer can heats up and steams the chicken from within, so you get a deliciously crisp outside and a succulent, beer-flavoured inside. When you take the lid of the barbecue off and your guests see a chicken akimbo on a tinny, they are going to be clucking wowed. Using a good local bird and a nice light ale can make your barbecue quite British. Of course, eating inside because it has started raining will always bring you back home as well. This is perfect barbecue food, served with lush salads, fresh bread and plenty of beer.

	FOR THE MARINADE:	
1 free-range chicken, about 1.8kg	1 tbsp salt	2 tbsp rapeseed oil
500ml can pale ale or lager	1 tbsp brown sugar	1 tsp black pepper
1 green chilli, split	big pinch each of ground paprika, coriander and cumin	1 tbsp vinegar
1 garlic clove, squashed		pinch of chopped thyme or rosemary
sprig of rosemary	2 garlic cloves, crushed	

1 The can inside the chicken makes the bird sit quite upright, so you need a barbecue with a lid big enough for it to fit under. A chicken stand is also quite useful to stop it wobbling, but you can manage without. This dish can also be done over an open grill, or in an oven at 180°C/Gas 4.

2 Combine all the seasonings for the marinade and rub over the chicken, inside and out. Leave in the fridge for at least 2 hours, or overnight if possible.

3 You want to cook the chicken on the barbecue indirectly (see page 140). This allows the chamber to get lovely and smoky, and because the meat is not directly on the flame it cooks slowly without burning. You want a barbecue temperature of around 200°C for this.

4 Crack open the can, take a big swig, then put the chilli, garlic and rosemary inside it. Shove the can up the chicken, getting it well inside. Place it upright in the barbecue, using the chicken stand if you have one. Place the lid on and cook for about 1½ hours until the chicken is crisp and tender. To check if the bird is done, either use a meat probe – you want a temperature of 75°C – or bend out the leg and look down the joint. It should pop away easily and be cooked through (no pink). Lift the chicken off its beer can and leave to rest for 20 minutes before cutting up. It's easy: all you need to do is use tongs and a fork to tease the meat off the joints and into delicious chunks.

BARBECUED BRISKET
··· SERVES 4–6 ···

Henry: Whether the sun is shining or not, it's time to step forward and reclaim our rightful stance at the helm of the good ship *Barbecue* and show everyone that we are better than a burnt raw sausage or flaccid Quorn burger. We are men! Men in control of our destiny! And we want beef, and lots of it!

2kg piece of boneless brisket (untrimmed)	**FOR A HOME-MADE STEAK RUB:**	10g onion flakes
50g Dijon mustard	20g sea salt (smoked if possible)	**FOR THE GLAZE:**
25ml Worcestershire sauce	10g dark brown sugar	1 bottle of beer
30g good steak rub (I like California Rancher – made in Bristol!) or make your own:	5g black pepper	50ml cider vinegar
	5g smoked paprika	30g brown sugar
	5g celery salt	20g steak rub
	5g cayenne pepper	10g tomato purée
	10g garlic flakes	20ml Worcester sauce

1 If making home-made steak rub, then mix the ingredients together and keep in a jar for barbecue needs.

2 Mix the glaze ingredients together in a bowl.

3 The day before beef time, take your hunk of cow and lay it on a board. Smear one side with mustard then douse with Worcestershire sauce. Sprinkle the steak rub over and massage into the meat. Turn over and repeat. Place into the fridge for at least a few hours if not overnight.

4 Heat the barbecue. This works best if your barbecue has a lid and a large grilling area. Get the grill working on one side and place the beef on the other side to cook it by the indirect method. A foil tray of water beneath the beef keeps things moist and steamy. Close the lid and give the meat at least 6 hours to do its magic.

5 After an hour or so, lift the lid off and check proceedings. Now for some moppin'. Using a pastry brush, slosh the sauce over the beef. This will give it an amazing crust and pimp the beef right up. Do this every hour or so until the beef is soft and giving with a dark glaze.

6 Remove the beef and let it rest for 20 minutes. Then, using a fork, just shred it into chunks and serve.

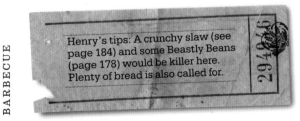

Henry's tips: A crunchy slaw (see page 184) and some Beastly Beans (page 178) would be killer here. Plenty of bread is also called for.

BARBECUE

OAK-PLANKED SMOKED HORSERADISH SALMON

··· SERVES 4 ···

Dan Cooper: The oak-plank method of barbecuing was, I believe, developed in the North Americas and British Colombia, where whole sides of salmon would be pegged to cedar planks and cooked in an upright fashion near a fire. The wood slightly smoulders and the moisture in it flavours the meat. Soak the oak plank and hickory chips (which you can get from a good barbecue supplier) in water for at least 2 hours, or overnight, before use. You might need to weight them down to keep them submerged.

1 pre-soaked oak plank	500g side of salmon	1 jar of good quality horseradish, or even better home-made
2 large handfuls of pre-soaked hickory wood chips	sea salt and coarsely ground black pepper	1 lemon

1 Cut the fish into four 125g fillets, removing the skin first and making sure there are no bones. (Or ask your fishmonger to do this.) Place the salmon fillets on the wet oak plank and salt them. With a basting brush, apply a thin layer of horseradish, and then add a good amount of black pepper.

2 Very thinly slice the lemon, and place 4 slices on top of each fillet.

3 Cook the oak-planked salmon by the indirect method (see page 140). Add the wood chips to the hot coals to the side, and cook for 20–25 minutes with the lid down until the flesh is flaky and the fish is golden on top.

BARBECUED BUTTERFLIED LAMB WITH CHILLI

··· SERVES 4–8 ···

The British are known the world over for roasting meat, and a roast is never better than when done over a real fire. It's a shame to see the barbecue as only for cooking burgers and sausages. This recipe is a great step up to doing larger joints barbecue-style.

1 leg of lamb, butterflied by your butcher	20g harissa paste	200ml Greek yogurt
	FOR THE YOGURT SAUCE:	a few mint leaves, finely chopped
20ml virgin pressed rapeseed oil	½ cucumber	salt and pepper
2 garlic cloves, chopped	2 garlic cloves	half a lemon

1 The night before the big day, prepare the lamb. Mix the oil, garlic and harissa, and season liberally with salt and pepper. Rub it all over the lamb, getting in all the nooks and crannies. Put into the fridge to marinate for at least a couple of hours.

2 The lamb will take around 30 minutes to cook on the barbecue until pink. Cook it over direct heat with the lid down (which helps prevent flare-ups, as well as ensuring it cooks well). Because the lamb is different thicknesses all over, it will cook more quickly in some parts than others; this gives you lovely pink meat with some crunchy bits. Remove and rest for at least 20 minutes before slicing up.

3 To make the yogurt sauce, peel the cucumber. Split in half lengthways and remove the seeds with a teaspoon. Grate the flesh into a bowl. Grate the garlic into the bowl with the cucumber, then add the yogurt and mint and season with salt and pepper. Squeeze in a little lemon juice and give it a stir. Thinly slice the lamb and serve it with the sauce.

LANCASHIRE LOLLIPOPS
··· MAKES 8 SMALL KEBABS OR 4 LARGE ONES ···

Lancashire lollipops are moreish **BBQ** sticks that celebrate all that is good from the county: Goosnargh chicken, potatoes, and a sweet sticky Blackpool marinade to give it some balls. When in Blackpool, do as Blackpool does, and eat portable, sweet, salty treats. This would be good with a watercress salad seasoned with lemon juice, olive oil and some diced red chilli.

FOR THE MARINADE:

1½ tsp smoked paprika

4 tbsp brown sugar

1 tbsp sea salt

3 garlic cloves, crushed

1 tsp coarsely ground black pepper

1 small bunch of thyme, leaves picked

4 sprigs of rosemary, leaves picked

1 x 500ml bottle of stout

2 tbsp black treacle

1 star anise

1 tbsp cornflour, dissolved in 3 tbsp water

TO MAKE THE LOLLIPOPS:

4 boneless skinless chicken breasts

300g new potatoes

2 red onions, quartered

8 short (or 4 long) skewers

1 Put all the marinade ingredients except the cornflour in a medium saucepan, stir well and set over a high heat. Bring to a gentle, rolling boil and cook for 5 minutes. Stir in the slaked cornflour and continue to cook and thicken for 3 minutes. Take off the heat and allow to cool to room temperature.

2 Chop each chicken breast into about 4 chunks and add to the cooled marinade.

3 Cut the larger new potatoes into similar-sized chunks to the chicken. Put on a saucepan of water, season with salt, and add the potatoes. Bring to the boil and simmer for 8–10 minutes. Drain in a colander and leave to dry out and cool down.

4 Build the lollipops in stages. Skewer the potatoes first, then add chicken, then an onion quarter, then potato, then chicken. Continue until you've finished all the skewers. Pour over the remaining marinade.

5 Put the kebabs on a hot griddle pan or barbecue and cook for about 15 minutes, turning and pressing down every few minutes. Serve hot.

BEASTLY BEANS

··· SERVES 8–10 ···

Henry: What could be better as a side for hot, sticky, smoky meat than some
kick-ass beans? These are full of flavour, rich and glossy. I've made a vegetarian
and a non-veggie version. The beans are perfect without the meat addition, but
as a butcher I can't help myself. If you're looking for that full-on meat experience,
this will certainly set you on your way. The meaty version takes three hours longer
to make, but the magic of the oxtail is that it will give the beans a deep meaty
flavour and the sauce unctuous body that is oh-my-goodness so amazing I just
want to eat a bowl right now.

2 tbsp oil	1 piece of cassia bark (sometimes mislabelled cinnamon, but it's much woodier)	3 x 400g tins haricot or cannellini beans, drained
2 onions, chopped		smoked sea salt and pepper
1 stick of celery, chopped	1 star anise	splash of sherry vinegar or red wine vinegar
1 red chilli, chopped	1 big squirt of tomato purée	
1 bulb of garlic, halved through the centre	2 tbsp veg. Worcestershire sauce	**NON-VEGGIE OPTION:**
	2 tbsp black treacle	2 tbsp duck fat
1 large sprig of rosemary, leaves picked and chopped	2 x 400g tins chopped tomatoes	4 rings of oxtail
1 tsp smoked paprika		200g thick-cut bacon, diced

1 Heat the oil in a large casserole pot,
add the onions and celery and sweat
for 5 minutes until nice and soft with a
little colour on the edges. Add the chilli,
garlic, rosemary and spices. Shizzle
them around the pot to get the onions
all coated.

2 Add the tomato purée, Worcestershire
sauce, treacle and tinned tomatoes.
Bring to a simmer and then add the beans.
You want the beans to be quite loose
in the pan, so add half a tin's worth of
water. Season the pot, cover and simmer
gently for around 30 minutes. Remove
the garlic bulb halves, and squeeze the
flesh back into the beans. Finish with
a splash of vinegar to bring out the
flavours and excite the palette.

3 For the non-vegetarian version, heat the duck fat in a large casserole pot. When hot, brown off the oxtail for about 3 minutes on each side. Remove and set aside.

4 Add the onions and celery and sweat for 3 minutes. Add the bacon to the pan and fry for a few minutes to colour them all up, then add the chilli, garlic, rosemary and spices and stir them all in. Add the tomato purée, Worcestershire sauce, treacle and tinned tomatoes. Bring to a simmer, then return the oxtail and add the beans. Add a whole tin's worth of water.

5 Season the pot and simmer gently for about 3 hours with the lid on until the meat on the oxtail is beautifully tender. Don't be tempted to finish cooking early, before the meat is tender. When it reaches perfection, pick the tail out and, using a fork, flake the meat off into the beans. Discard the bone. Remove the garlic bulb halves and squeeze the flesh back into the pot. Have a final stir and season, with a splash of vinegar to finish.

Henry's tips: Cook the beans on the cool side of the barbecue so they can take on the smoky aromas.

These beans are best eaten a little cooler than piping hot.

294046

BARBECUED AUBERGINE, FRESH GARLIC, LEMON AND MINT SALAD

··· SERVES 3–6 ···

Henry: I adore aubergines. I find them both beautiful and delicious: the tight purple jacket and, when cooked, the amazingly soft, meaty flesh. On the other hand, badly cooked they can be dire. The thought of *al dente* aubergine makes my skin crawl. By cooking them on the barbecue you get that wonderful smoky flavour, and if you cook them alongside other stuff it makes use of the heat.

3 aubergines	2 garlic cloves	few sprigs of mint, leaves picked and chopped
1 tsp virgin olive oil	2 tbsp virgin olive oil	
salt and pepper	1 tsp sherry vinegar or lemon juice	1 tsp black onion seeds

1 Cut the aubergines in half lengthways. Score the flesh in a criss-cross fashion. Rub with oil and season. Place skin-side down on the barbecue and cover with the lid. Cook on gentle coals for 10–15 minutes or until the aubergine is soft and giving with a crisp outside. Remove and set aside.

2 Quickly grate the garlic into a small bowl and add the olive oil, sherry vinegar or lemon juice, mint, onion seeds and seasoning. Mix together and drizzle over the aubergine. All the dressing will sink into the soft flesh, giving it a fresh, sharp zing.

COLESLAWS

Henry: Ain't nothing fresher than a crunchy slaw. Definitely the
salad of the moment, and with good reason. With a sharp knife and
some spanking ingredients you can quickly make some beautiful
salads. When making a slaw it's always better to use a larger bowl
than you think at first you need, because until you have tamed
the salad it can be quite unruly and difficult to stir without
it making friends with your kitchen floor.

RETRO SLAW
··· SERVES 6–8 ···

A homemade slaw is miles apart and a billion times better than any bought version.

1 white cabbage, thinly sliced (a mandolin gets it extra fine)	2 shallots, finely diced	1 tsp white wine vinegar or lemon juice
2 carrots, grated	3 tbsp mayonnaise or crème fraîche	salt and pepper

1 Mix all the vegetables together. Just before serving, add the mayo or crème fraîche and vinegar, and season.

PIMPING
The best thing about a slaw is that it's easy to add new ingredients and make it completely different. Here are some ideas.

chopped green chilli

herbs: parsley, tarragon, mint, chervil, and so on

pomegranate seeds, dried cranberries, apricots and other dried fruit

fresh fruit, such as orange, apple, pear

seeds: toasted sesame, pumpkin, poppy, black onion, among others

nuts: walnuts, hazelnuts, almonds, pecans, and more

fennel, radishes, celeriac, red onion, peppers, red cabbage, beetroot

capers, olives

DRESSINGS

chilli mayonnaise: see page 150

mustard mayonnaise: 4 tbsp mayo mixed with 1 tbsp grain mustard and a grind of pepper

crème fraîche, lemon juice, salt and pepper

yogurt, garlic and mint

RETRO OX TONGUE
AND TARRAGON SLAW
··· SERVES 6–8 ···

Henry: I made this meaty number in the summer for a pop-up Tom and I did for thirty guests in the SVA train goods shed in Stroud. It was a night of beef, bread and tango, so it seemed fitting to put beef in the salad. Using the retro slaw base I added sliced ox tongue, with tarragon to spike it. The result was so delicious that I've been eating it ever since.

200g ox tongue, around 4 slices	1 tbsp capers
small bunch of tarragon	retro slaw (facing page)

1 Slice the ox tongue into matchsticks, chop the tarragon and mix with the capers through the slaw. Easy!

CELERIAC, APPLE AND CAPERS WITH MUSTARD

··· SERVES 6–8 ···

A beautifully pale slaw that is full on in flavour and works well with pâtés, smoked fish and cured meats.

1 large or 2 small celeriac	1 tsp fine capers	big pinch of chopped parsley
2 crunchy green apples	2 tbsp mayonnaise	salt and pepper
1 shallot	1 tsp grain mustard	

1 Celeriac can be a daunting and gnarly-looking vegetable. Don't be afraid: behind its warty exterior is a delicious root vegetable that is great mashed, roasted or raw. Peel the celeriac and using either a knife or a mandolin slice as thinly as possible into rounds. Stack a small pile and cut the disks into matchsticks. Place into a bowl.

2 Cut the apple into slices. Don't peel as it looks beautiful with some colour. Stop when you get to the core. Cut the slices into matchsticks and add to the celeriac. Dice the shallot and add with all the remaining ingredients. Give it a mix. The celeriac will take around 15 minutes to soften, so make it a little ahead of time.

FENNEL, RADISH, WHITE CABBAGE, WALNUTS AND CHERVIL WITH A YOGURT DRESSING

··· SERVES 6–8 ···

Delicious as a simple salad or served with lots of items on a barbecue.

4 fennel bulbs	50g walnuts, toasted	salt and pepper
1 bunch of radishes	small bunch of chervil, chopped	**FOR THE DRESSING:**
1 small white cabbage	juice of 1 lemon	1 garlic clove
1 red onion	20ml extra virgin olive oil	100ml natural yogurt

1 Slice the fennel crossways – that makes it easier to eat. The thinner the better. Do the same to the radishes and cabbage. Put in a large bowl. Dice the red onion and crush the walnuts. Mix through the salad with most of the chopped chervil (reserve some for the dressing), lemon juice, oil and seasoning.

2 To make the dressing, grate or chop the garlic and stir through the yogurt with a pinch of chervil. Season. Drizzle artfully over the slaw and serve.

BARBECUED PILCHARDS WITH PEACH AND MINT SALAD

··· SERVES 4 ···

This is a great summer dish, perfect on a hot day. The mint and the peach salad are very good with the oily pilchards. Pilchards are a Cornish fish, similar to sardines.

8 whole pilchards, gutted	6 peaches	1 chilli, diced
extra virgin olive oil	200g rocket	handful of mint, chopped
salt and pepper	1 shallot, finely sliced	half a lemon

1 Rub the skin of the pilchards with olive oil and season them. Halve and stone the peaches, and cut into wedges. Grill the pilchards over direct heat for 2–3 minutes on each side. At the same time, grill the peaches just to char the outside, without cooking them.

2 Mix the grilled peach wedges in a salad bowl with rocket, shallot, chilli and mint, and season with olive oil, salt and pepper and a few squeezes of lemon. Toss together and serve with the pilchards.

Henry's tip: White peaches are my favourite, and very good on the barbecue. They have a floral scent, a subtle flavour and they are really sweet.

CHILLI SQUID WITH ROCKET AND AIOLI

··· SERVES 3–6, DEPENDING ON APPETITE ···

Super-fast, and delicious too, this makes a big bowl. Your own home-made aioli will make it super-special. Aioli is a strong, garlic mayonnaise. Purists say it should be just garlic, lemon and extra virgin oil, but this will sting your mouth. I go for the less hard-core version. The aioli will last for a week in your fridge.

6 medium-sized prepared squids from the fishmonger	salt and pepper	1 squeeze of lemon
2 garlic cloves	big bunch of rocket, trimmed	1 egg yolk
2 red chillies	lemon	50ml vegetable oil
olive oil	**FOR THE AIOLI:**	50ml extra virgin olive oil
	4 garlic cloves	

1 For aioli, grate the garlic cloves into a round-bottomed bowl, then add the lemon and yolk. Whisk together, then slowly add the oils, drip by drip, while continuing to whisk. This will emulsify with the yolk and the oil to make a thick mayo-like sauce. When all the oil is added, taste for seasoning. Thin with a splash of cold water if it's a touch thick.

2 Place the squid tentacles in a big bowl. Cut the squid tube in half lengthways so it's flat, and carefully score the outside in a crisscross fashion to enable the flavour to penetrate. Put in the bowl with the tentacles. Chop the garlic and chilli and mix into the squid with enough olive oil to moisten them, and salt and pepper to taste. Leave to marinade for 30 minutes.

3 Heat the barbecue to blisteringly hot. Put the rocket in a serving bowl and dress with lemon juice and olive oil. Flash-grill the squid for no more than 2 minutes, otherwise it will become tough and chewy. Toss into the dressed rocket leaves, and serve immediately with a big dish of aioli.

BARBECUE SAUCE

··· MAKES ABOUT 750ML ···

Dan Cooper: Top sauce for BBQing days.

1 tbsp olive oil	2 tsp smoked paprika	2 tbsp Worcestershire sauce
2 garlic cloves, crushed	1 tsp chilli powder	salt and pepper
3cm fresh root ginger, grated	230g dark muscovado sugar	4 large handfuls of hickory wood chips, for smoking (optional)
1 shallot, finely chopped	2 tbsp Golden Syrup	
1 tsp allspice	400g tinned tomatoes	
1 tsp mustard powder	280ml cider vinegar	

1 Warm the oil in a saucepan over a medium heat, then add the garlic, ginger and shallot and cook for 2–3 minutes until golden. Add the allspice, mustard powder, smoked paprika and chilli powder and cook through for 1 minute, stirring continuously. Add the sugar and syrup and stir for 30 seconds, allowing the caramel flavours to develop. Finally add the passata, vinegar and Worcestershire sauce. Bring the sauce up to a gentle simmer and cook, uncovered, for 10–15 minutes until it has thickened. Allow to cool a little, then, using a hand-held blender or a liquidizer, blitz the sauce until smooth. Season with salt and pepper.

2 If you wish to smoke the sauce to develop a stronger, more complex flavour, transfer it to a wide, shallow, heatproof dish to increase the surface area. Smoke the sauce in a covered barbecue using hickory wood chips and by the indirect method (see page 140), keeping the temperature low. If you're using charcoal, use only half a chimney starter full. Smoke for as long as you wish to achieve your desired smokiness; about 1 hour and 30 minutes is ideal.

BARBECUE BANANA AND RUM UPSIDE-DOWN TART

··· SERVES 4 ···

Dan Cooper: This is a take on the recipe said to have been invented by the sisters Tatin in France. We've substituted banana and rum for the apple of the original, and ramped it up with a bit of outdoor cooking. No longer the innocent and respectable dessert it once was.

4 bananas	85g dark brown sugar, plus extra for sprinkling	50ml dark rum
60g butter, plus 10g for the top of the tart	juice of half a lemon	8 cloves
		½ sheet ready-made puff pastry

1 Cut the bananas into 2.5cm-thick slices.

2 Melt the butter, sugar, lemon juice and rum in a 16cm heavy-based pan (no plastic or wood handles). Stir occasionally with a wooden spoon until the sugar has dissolved and the caramel is bubbling. This can be done on a side burner or on the grill. Take off the heat.

3 Using a pestle and mortar, crush the cloves and sprinkle on to the caramel. Arrange the banana slices in the caramel in a snug, even pattern.

4 Place the pastry securely on top of the bananas so it forms a tight lid for the pan. Sprinkle with a little dark brown sugar, and distribute the 10g butter evenly over the top.

5 Bake indirect (see page 140) in the covered barbecue for 20–25 minutes until the pastry is golden brown. Allow to cool for 5 minutes before turning out. Place a serving dish over the pan and flip upside down to release the dessert, so that the pastry is underneath. Allow to cool for several minutes before serving.

DINNER

HENRY

This is the big meal of the day for me and it's where I put the most effort in. I feel it should be sat down to and enjoyed, not eaten in front of the telly. It's the time when you talk about your day.

TOM

You cook these when you're welcoming someone home or opening your house to guests. To ramp it up a bit for a special occasion, there's the venison haunch and pigeon Wellington.

SMUGGLERS' PIE
JERUSALEM ARTICHOKE, PRUNE AND CREAM BAKE
TORY COBBLER
TOAD IN THE HOLE
SHEPHERD'S PIE
SMOKED FISH PIE
STEAK PIE
TRI-PIE
SWEETCORN WITH GARLIC MASH
MEGA MASH-UP
BEETROOT TART WITH GOAT'S CHEESE
PIGEON WELLINGTON
RARE ROAST TOPSIDE WITH WARM JERSEY ROYAL SALAD
BEST-EVER GLAZED CARROTS
VENISON HAUNCH WITH SWEET AND SOUR ONIONS
CHICKEN AND LEEK PIE
GRILLED YOUNG LEEKS WITH CHOPPED EGG DRESSING
ROASTED PUMPKIN WITH SEEDS
ASPARAGUS WITH GREEN SAUCE

SMUGGLERS' PIE

··· MAKES 4 ···

In Exmouth we were taken out in a boat by shanty singers, who told us about the old smuggling tradition. One of the most popular goods to smuggle was brandy; it was a luxury item and highly taxed, so this was a way round paying the duty. An onshore beacon was used to guide the smugglers in to land. Instead of using red wine or ale for the beef in this pie, we used cider, with a lighter result. We then topped it with mashed potato, teased up into a peak, and for a bit of theatre we flambéed it at the table in apple brandy so it lit up like a smugglers' beacon.

FOR THE FILLING:

1kg diced beef (chuck or skirt), cut into medium-sized pieces

40g flour

salt and pepper

1–2 tbsp rapeseed oil

1 onion, diced

2 carrots, diced

2 garlic cloves

500ml cider

small bunch of thyme, leaves picked

3 bay leaves

200ml dark beef stock

1 tbsp tomato purée

FOR THE SHORTCRUST PASTRY:

250g plain flour

pinch of salt

125g cold butter, cubed

1 tbsp ice-cold water

FOR THE MASH:

800g Maris Piper potatoes, peeled and chopped

2 apples, peeled and chopped

splash of warm milk

1 egg yolk

salt and pepper

knob of butter

TO FLAMBÉ:

80ml apple brandy

1 Heat the oven to 170°C/Gas 3. Dust the beef in flour and season it. Heat 1 tablespoon of oil in an ovenproof pan or casserole over a high heat and sear the beef until browned – do this in batches if necessary to avoid overcrowding the pan. (Overcrowding the pan will reduce the temperature and cause the meat to stew more than sear.) Remove with a slotted spoon and drain on kitchen paper.

2 Reduce the heat to medium and add the onion, carrot and garlic. Fry for 3–4 minutes, until softened, adding a little more oil if required. Return the browned beef along with the cider, thyme, bay leaves, beef stock and tomato purée. Bring the mixture to a simmer. Put the lid on the pan, transfer to the oven and cook for 1½ to 2 hours until the beef is tender. Taste to check the seasoning, then set aside to cool completely.

3 To make the pastry, put the flour and salt in a bowl. Rub in the butter cubes until the mixture resembles breadcrumbs. Add enough of the cold water to bring the dough together. Wrap the dough in cling film and chill for 20 minutes.

4 Heat the oven to 190°C/Gas 5. Put a baking tray in the oven to heat up. Take 4 individual pie dishes of about 500ml capacity. Divide the pastry into 4, and roll out to fill the bases of the pie dishes. Trim the edges. Fill with the slow-cooked beef.

5 For the mash, put the potatoes in a saucepan, cover with water, bring to the boil then simmer for 10 minutes. Add the apple and continue to simmer for another 10 minutes. Drain and return to the hot saucepan to steam off any remaining liquid. Add the warm milk, egg yolk and seasoning, and mash well. Divide between the pies, forking the mash up into beacon shapes. Dot with butter.

6 Put the pies on the hot tray in the oven and bake for 25–30 minutes, until golden-brown and bubbling on top. For the full effect, ignite the brandy in a ladle and pour over the mash 'beacons'. The room will fill with the wafting smells of brandy, beef and apples.

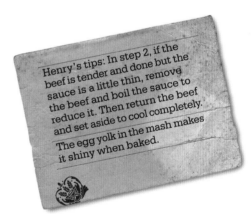

Henry's tips: In step 2, if the beef is tender and done but the sauce is a little thin, remove the beef and boil the sauce to reduce it. Then return the beef and set aside to cool completely.

The egg yolk in the mash makes it shiny when baked.

JERUSALEM ARTICHOKE, PRUNE AND CREAM BAKE

··· SERVES 4 ···

A beautiful creamy bake that is perfect in the dark of the colder months.
Delicious with any meaty pie.

2 tbsp butter	50g prunes, stones removed if necessary	100ml milk
2 shallots, sliced		100ml double cream
1 garlic clove, crushed	splash of Armagnac if you're feeling rich	salt and pepper
a sprig of thyme		500g Jerusalem artichokes

1 Heat the oven to 170°C/Gas 3. In a small saucepan melt the butter. Add the shallots and garlic and sweat for 2–3 minutes. Stir in the thyme and the prunes. If using the Armagnac, add it now and quickly either flambé or reduce it. Add the milk and cream and season.

2 No need to peel the Jerusalem artichokes, just give them a good scrub, then slice into thin discs. Place in a baking dish, pour over the creamy prunes and cover with foil. Bake for 30 minutes, then remove the foil and brown the top for 15 minutes. The bake should be brown and gorgeous on top with tender artichokes within.

TORY COBBLER
··· SERVES 8 ···

The Cotswolds is a Tory stronghold, and game shooting is an important countryside activity, making pheasant a shoo-in for the meat dish on our Bourton trip. It's possible to get good local English white wine in these parts too.

FOR THE STEW:

1.5kg pheasant, de-boned (ask your butcher to do this) and cut into bite-sized pieces

40g plain flour

salt and pepper

2 tbsp rapeseed oil

30g unsalted butter

1 large onion, roughly chopped

3 garlic cloves, roughly chopped

250g chestnut mushrooms, whole and cleaned

few sprigs of thyme

200ml white wine

1–2 tsp Tewkesbury (or English) mustard, to taste

500ml chicken stock

100g crème fraîche

FOR THE COBBLERS:

200g plain flour, plus extra for dusting

1 tsp baking powder

pinch of sea salt

200g cold unsalted butter, cubed

150g rolled oats

2 tbsp chopped flat-leaf parsley

a few leaves of sage, chopped

1 tsp Tewkesbury (or English) mustard

salt and pepper

1 free-range egg, beaten

50–100ml warm water

egg wash: 1 egg beaten with a pinch of salt

1 For the cobblers, put the flour, baking powder and salt into a bowl. Rub in the butter until you have a breadcrumb-like texture. Stir in the oats, parsley, sage and mustard, and season. Use the egg and as much of the warm water as you need to bind the mixture together. Shape into 24 roughly even balls and put in the fridge to firm up.

2 Heat the oven to 200°C/Gas 6. Dust the pheasant in flour and season it. Heat 1 tablespoon of the oil in an ovenproof pan or casserole over a high heat. Brown the pheasant in batches.

3 In a separate pan, on a low heat, melt the butter and add the remaining oil. Fry the onion gently until golden. Turn the heat up, add the garlic, mushrooms and thyme, and fry for a further 1–2 minutes.

4 Deglaze the pheasant pan with the wine and scrape the bottom to get the nice pheasant bits. Reduce the wine by about half, then add the mixture from the mushroom pan, along with the mustard, to taste, and the stock. Return the browned pheasant. Bring slowly to the boil, then simmer for 5 minutes. Stir in the crème fraîche, and taste to check the seasoning.

5 Arrange the dumplings on top of the pheasant stew and brush them with egg wash. Put the stew in the hot oven, uncovered, and cook for 15–20 minutes or until the dumplings are crisp and golden.

DINNER

TOAD IN THE HOLE

··· FEEDS 4 BIG BOYS ···

Henry: I make the sausage side happen here, so if Tom wants a slice of the action he has to make the batter. This batter makes the best, most foolproof Yorkies. The only thing to consider is having a very hot oven. I like a herby Lincolnshire sausage but any will do so long as it's of a good quality. Best of all, make your own (see page 35).

a little rapeseed oil, for frying	sprigs of thyme, leaves picked	275ml milk
8 fat sausages	1 pinch of fennel seeds	275ml soda water
2 garlic cloves	**FOR THE YORKSHIRE PUDDING:**	275g flour
2 red onions	5 free-range eggs	1 tsp salt

1 First job, make the batter. It's always better when it sits for an hour or so. In a large bowl whisk the eggs then add the milk and soda water. The soda water helps to aerate the batter, giving it extra lift. I don't agree with baking powder, however – this in my mind is cheating. Slowly add the flour and salt, whisking the whole time so you don't get lumps. When it's all smooth and thick like double cream, leave to one side.

2 Heat the oven to 200°C/Gas 6. Now heat the baking pan you plan to cook the toad in, on the hob. This saves on washing up later (so long as the pan you use is flameproof). Add a splash of oil and carefully brown the sausages on all sides. Meanwhile, slice the garlic and cut the onions into wedges. Add to the browned sausages with the thyme and fennel seeds. Fry for 5 minutes until the onions have started to soften.

3 Now for the crucial bit. The sausages are not cooked, but don't panic as they will finish off in the oven. While the pan is still hot, pour in the batter. It should splutter around the edges. Quickly place in the oven and shut the door. Bake for 15 minutes without peeking. We don't want a flat hole. After 15 minutes, take a look at the situation. Hopefully it's beautifully risen but still quite pale. Opening the door lets the steam out and allows the batter to crisp up. It should take only 5 minutes more.

Henry's tip: Eat hot, with lots of mustard and some onion gravy.

SHEPHERD'S PIE
··· SERVES 6 ···

Henry: I won over students with this one in our pie-off. The thing I did differently to a classic shepherd's pie was to give it a dash of Worcestershire sauce, and cooked the meat with a bit of red wine. It did the trick. Good old-school British food. (I don't like to use leftover roast lamb, which is the traditional version.)

olive oil	2 large glasses of red wine	**FOR THE TOPPING:**
2 onions, diced	500ml chicken or beef stock	1kg Desiree potatoes, peeled and cubed
4 garlic cloves, sliced	good splash of Worcestershire sauce	50g butter
2 carrots, chopped		100ml milk
2 sticks of celery, chopped	2 tbsp tomato purée	1 egg yolk
2 sprigs of rosemary, leaves picked	splash of sherry vinegar	a few sprigs of rosemary, for decoration
750g good-quality lamb mince	salt and pepper	

1 Heat the oven to 200°C/Gas 6. Heat some olive oil in a large pan and add the onion, garlic, carrot, celery and rosemary. Cook on a medium heat for about 10 minutes until sweet and soft.

2 Add the lamb mince and cook until brown, then add the red wine and simmer down.

3 Add the stock, Worcestershire sauce, tomato purée and vinegar, season with salt and pepper, and simmer down until almost all the liquid has disappeared: about 45 minutes.

4 Meanwhile, boil the potatoes until soft, then drain and allow to steam dry in the colander for a few minutes. Melt the butter in a saucepan with the milk. Mash the potatoes until smooth then add the hot milk mixture, egg yolk and seasoning, and beat until smooth.

5 Put the lamb mixture into a deep casserole or pie dish and top with the mashed potato. Poke little sprigs of rosemary into the top of the mash, then bake in the hot oven for 35–40 minutes.

SMOKED FISH PIE

··· SERVES 6 ···

Tom: I made this for students, and they were hungover, and I reckon that's why they went for Henry's shepherd's pie over my fish pie. We grew up on fish pie. Charlie the fish man would come on a Friday and we'd always have fish pie. I wanted to revisit it and make it a bit more special, a bit less everyday. I made a white sauce using beer – so it's more a beige sauce – and mixed it with watercress. I put an Arbroath Smokie on the top to give it smokiness, and put horseradish in the mashed potato to give it zing. Good, comforting food with loads of flavour. I made waves on top of the mash using the back of a spoon to give it texture and crunch.

700ml milk	1 Arbroath Smokie or other smoked haddock, flaked	2 large handfuls of watercress, thick stalks removed
a few peppercorns		
zest of 1 lemon	small bunch of parsley, leaves picked and chopped	**FOR THE TOPPING:**
1 bay leaf		1kg Desiree potatoes, peeled and cubed
400g skinless salmon fillet, cut into chunks	2 tbsp (30g) butter	
	2 tbsp (30g) plain flour	50g butter
400g skinless white fish fillet, such as cod, cut into chunks	150ml beer	100ml milk
	salt and pepper	1 egg yolk
100g cooked prawns		2 tbsp grated horseradish

1 Heat the oven to 200°C/Gas 6. First, prepare the topping. Boil the potatoes until soft, then drain and allow to steam dry in the colander. Melt the butter in a saucepan with the milk. Mash the potatoes until smooth then beat in the hot milk, egg yolk and seasoning. Stir in the horseradish. Set aside but keep it warm.

2 Heat the milk with the peppercorns, lemon zest and bay leaf, then add the salmon and the white fish and gently poach for 2–3 minutes until it has lost its raw appearance. Use a slotted spoon to remove the fish and put it in a casserole or pie dish. Keep the milk for the sauce in step 4.

3 Add the prawns and haddock to the fish. Sprinkle with parsley.

4 In another pan, heat the butter and when it starts to foam add the flour and mix with a wooden spoon to form a roux. Cook for a couple of minutes, then add the beer, stirring all the time as it thickens. Add the milk you used to poach the fish, ladle by ladle until you have a thick smooth sauce. Season with salt and pepper. Stir in the watercress and allow to wilt for 30 seconds.

5 Pour the sauce over the fish, then cover the whole surface with the mash, using the back of a spoon to create waves. Bake in the hot oven for 30 minutes until the potato is golden.

STEAK PIE

··· SERVES 4 ···

Henry: Another winning pie. This is your Desperate Dan pie. It's big, and there's very little veg going on. It's all about the meat and the sauce, enriched by the marrow bone, which sticks out of the middle to make it extra manly. As it cooks, the marrow goes into the sauce. This was made for triathletes. What do you want after you've done some serious training? Do you want Tom's mashed potato and turnip pie? No, you want beef!

good glug of olive oil	2 big pinches of plain flour	**FOR THE SUET CRUST PASTRY:**
2 onions, chopped	250ml good red wine, such as a Cabernet Sauvignon	250g plain flour, plus extra for dusting
2 garlic cloves, sliced	500ml good-quality beef stock	125g beef suet
good pinch of fresh thyme leaves	500ml cold water	pinch of salt
1 star anise	1 piece marrow bone (optional)	125ml cold milk
1kg beef chuck, shin or cheek, diced	egg wash: 1 egg beaten with a pinch of salt	
salt and pepper		

1 First, make the pastry. Put the flour, suet and salt into a bowl and mix to combine. Add the cold milk to bring it all together into a dough. Wrap the dough in cling film and chill in the fridge for 30 minutes.

2 Put a large saucepan on the hob. When hot, pour in enough olive oil to just cover the base. Add the onions and fry for a few minutes until softened. Stir in the garlic, thyme leaves and star anise, then add the beef, season well and allow to brown – don't be tempted to stir. After 3 minutes or so, turn the beef and let it brown on the other side.

3 Stir in the flour, followed by the red wine. Boil for a couple of minutes to burn off the alcohol, then pour in the beef stock and the water. Turn the heat down, put the lid on and let it simmer for 4 hours or until the beef is tender. Spoon into a pie dish and allow to cool down.

4 Heat the oven to 190°C/Gas 5. When the pie mixture is cool, nestle the bone in the centre.

5 Roll the pastry on a lightly floured surface until large enough to cover the pie. Cut a cross in the middle to let the steam out. Brush the edge of the pie dish with egg wash so the pastry sticks, and put the pastry over the top of the pie, allowing the bone, if you've used it, to stick out. Using a fork, crimp the edge of the pie and carefully cut any overhanging pastry off. Liberally brush the top of the pie with egg wash and bake for 40 minutes until golden.

TRI-PIE

··· SERVES 6 ···

Tom: I made this for the Bristol triathletes. It needed to have a lot of sustenance and be very filling, and I wanted it to have some good healthy vegetables as well. I decided to layer up meat and two veg in a pie. It looks stunning when you cut into it. I was gutted to lose out on this one.

FOR THE SUET CRUST PASTRY:

500g plain flour

250g beef suet

good pinch of salt

250ml cold milk

FOR THE FIRST LAYER:

1kg shin of beef, diced

good pinch of plain flour

salt and pepper

knob of butter

1 carrot, diced

1 stick of celery, diced

5 shallots, peeled

2 sprigs of rosemary

2 sprigs of thyme

1 bay leaf

250ml beef stock

250ml ale

FOR THE SECOND LAYER:

3 medium potatoes, peeled and cut into chunks

3 turnips, peeled and cut into chunks

knob of butter

salt and pepper

pinch of thyme leaves

FOR THE THIRD LAYER:

knob of butter

2 heads of spring greens, shredded

zest of 1 lemon

salt and pepper

TO FINISH:

egg wash: 1 egg beaten with a pinch of salt

pinch of fresh thyme leaves

1 Mix the flour, suet and salt together in a bowl. Add the cold milk and bring it all together into a dough. Wrap in cling film and chill in the fridge for 30 minutes.

2 For the first layer of filling, dust the shin of beef with flour, then season it. Put the butter into a large, hot pan and add the carrot, celery, whole shallots, rosemary, thyme and bay leaf, and fry for 2–3 minutes. Add the seasoned meat and fry until brown, turning it over once to brown the other side. Add the beef stock and the ale, season again, cover and leave to simmer gently for 3 hours.

3 For the second layer, cook the potatoes and turnips until soft. (Separately, because they won't take the same amount of time.) Test with a knife point for tenderness, then drain, put in a bowl and add butter, salt and pepper and thyme. Mash them well.

4 For the final layer, melt the butter in a frying pan, add the greens, zest and seasoning and wilt for 5 minutes.

5 Heat the oven to 200°C/Gas 6. Roll out the suet crust pastry to 5mm thin and tease it into a cake tin of 22–23cm diameter, covering the base and extending up the sides. Now layer the pie: beef, then potato, then the greens. Fold the pastry in over the top, brush with egg wash and sprinkle with thyme. Bake for 1 hour until golden.

SWEETCORN WITH GARLIC MASH

··· SERVES 4 ···

These are great with the venison haunch on page 216.

FOR THE GARLIC MASH:

1kg Desiree potatoes or other mashers, peeled and halved

4 garlic cloves

100ml milk

150g butter

salt and pepper

FOR THE SWEETCORN:

1 corn on the cob

1 tsp oil

salt

1 tbsp butter

sprig of rosemary, leaves picked and chopped

1 Make the mash as on the facing page. The only difference is to cook the garlic in with the spuds (plus I've gone a bit lighter on the butter here).

2 Take the corn cob and rub a little oil and salt on the kernels. Fire up a gas hob and carefully char the outside. Use tongs or gloves to turn the cob. You want nicely browned corn for that sweet charred taste. Then cut the corn kernels off with a sharp knife. If should be cooked but not mushy.

3 Heat a frying pan and foam the butter with the rosemary. Add the sweet corn, season and cook for 4 minutes. It should be glossy, buttery and delicious. Serve with the garlic mash alongside the venison or other roast meats.

MEGA MASH-UP

··· SERVES 4 ···

If you get your mash right, it can be a thing of buttery beauty. There are just a few things to consider first. Get the right spud: something like a Desiree, the one with the red jacket, is perfect. Use plenty of butter and a splash of hot milk. Work fast so it stays hot; as it cools, the mash will go gloopy and starchy.

1kg Desiree spuds	200g butter	
100ml milk	salt and pepper	

1 Cut the spuds in half, but don't peel. Place in a pan of cold water and bring to a simmer. We leave the jacket on as this helps keep the spud from falling apart. We also cook the spud in large chunks so that less surface area is in contact with the water, which keeps the starch in the spud, where it belongs.

2 Simmer gently for 25 minutes until the spud is tender. Drain in a colander and leave to steam. Now, a mouli-legumes or a potato ricer is best here because it removes the skin as it mashes. If you only have a masher, you will have to peel first.

3 Give the pan a quick clean, add the milk and butter and put back on the heat. Having everything hot makes for better mash.

4 Add the mash to the pan and beat vigorously with a wooden spoon. Season generously and serve straight away. If you want to be naughty, add another 100g of butter for extra luxury.

BEETROOT TART
WITH GOAT'S CHEESE
··· SERVES 4–6 ···

Tom: I was asked to create a recipe for a beetroot lovers' website, and I was stumped, but Henry said, 'Do a beetroot tarte Tatin,' as if it was the most obvious idea in the world. I have to say it was delicious.

75g golden caster sugar	1 tbsp honey, plus extra to serve	250g ready-made puff pastry
sea salt	6 sprigs of thyme, leaves picked	flour for dusting
40g butter	4 cooked beetroot	4–8 discs or wedges of goat's cheese
splash of sherry vinegar	black pepper	

1 Heat the oven to 180°C/Gas 4. In a smallish ovenproof frying pan over a medium heat, heat the sugar until it dissolves, then add a big pinch of sea salt, the butter and a splash of sherry vinegar, and keep stirring. It'll go foamy. Keep stirring on the heat until it has gone a mahogany brown. Take great care not to burn yourself – use oven gloves and don't let the sugar catch and burn. Take off the heat and stir in the honey and thyme.

2 Cut the beetroot into nice fat slices and carefully (so you don't burn your fingers) arrange the slices fanned out over the caramel, working in a spiral towards the centre. Use all the beetroot up. Season with a pinch of salt and a twist of pepper.

3 On a lightly floured work surface, roll out the puff pastry large enough to cover the beetroot. Place it on top of the beetroot, tucking the edges down into the pan. Put the whole lot into the oven and bake for about 30 minutes until the pastry is golden. Remove from the oven and let the pan cool down just a little.

4 Get a plate that's bigger than the pan and invert it over the pan. Holding the two together, and using oven gloves, turn the whole lot over. Leave it for 30 seconds for all the caramel to fall from the pan on to the top of the tart, then whip the pan off.

5 Serve by the wedge while still warm, with goat's cheese on top, and, if you fancy it, a drizzle of honey and a few extra thyme leaves.

PIGEON WELLINGTON
··· SERVES 4 ···

If you're having a dinner party and you want to impress with a knock-out starter, this will be a show-stopper. It may sound daunting but get all the basics right and you will be on easy street. Beetroot remoulade is a kind of slaw. It goes well with the pigeon and looks very pretty. A nice green salad also goes very well with this.

1 tsp butter	salt and pepper	**FOR THE REMOULADE:**
1 garlic clove, crushed	splash of rapeseed oil, for frying	2 large cooked beetroot
1 sprig of thyme	4 plump pigeon breasts	1 tbsp crème fraîche
100g button mushrooms, chopped	handful of large spinach leaves	1 tsp horseradish
4 chestnuts or 20g hazelnuts, finely chopped	200g ready-made all-butter puff pastry	half a lemon
drip of truffle oil (optional)	egg wash: 1 egg beaten with a pinch of salt	salt and pepper
pinch of chopped parsley		

1 Heat a small pan and melt the butter. Add the crushed garlic and the thyme sprig, and fry for a minute or so, then add the mushrooms and cook until they've coloured and most of their moisture has gone: about 10 minutes. Then stir in the chestnuts or hazelnuts, the truffle oil (if using) and parsley. Season and set aside to cool.

2 Heat a frying pan and add a splash of oil. Season the pigeon breasts all over and quickly sear in the pan to colour them, not cook through: about 45 seconds each side. Remove and allow to cool.

3 Heat a small pan of water. When boiling, plunge the spinach in, then take it straight out again with a slotted spoon and into a bowl of cold water. This cooks it but retains the vibrant colour. Remove from the cold water and gently squeeze out any excess moisture. Open out the leaves and allow them to air.

4 Using a sharp knife, carefully cut an opening in the pigeon breasts to make a pocket. Spoon in some mushrooms and close the breast back up. Now carefully wrap each breast in spinach so it is completely covered. Place in the fridge to firm up for 15 minutes.

5 Roll out the pastry until it is about 2mm thick and cut out 4 discs that are each roughly twice the size of the pigeon breasts. Place a breast on each disc, slightly off-centre. Brush the edges with egg wash and fold the longer side over the breast, making sure it is nice and tight around the meat with a neat rim on one side. Using a fork, crimp the edges and trim off excess pastry. Place in the fridge for 30 minutes, or until needed.

6 Heat the oven to 220°C/Gas 7 and put in a baking tray to get hot.

7 Slice the beetroot, then stack the slices and cut across into fine matchsticks. Put into a bowl. Mix the crème fraîche and horseradish with a squeeze of lemon and season to taste. Stir into the beetroot. The remoulade should be beautifully pink and deliver a small horseradish kick.

8 Take the pigeon Wellingtons from the fridge, brush with egg wash and place directly on the hot baking tray. This will stop them from getting soggy bottoms. Bake for 9–12 minutes until the pastry is golden and crisp. The pigeon will still be nice and pink inside.

9 Allow to rest for 4 minutes, then carefully, with your sharpest knife, slice in half or threes. Place on plates and serve with a spoon of beetroot remoulade.

Henry's tip: If you have the pigeon bones, brown them in a pan with a splash of oil and some chopped onion, carrot and garlic. Add wine and a dark stock, and simmer with a sprig of thyme for an hour. Pass through a sieve and reduce in a pan until nice and intense. Season and spoon over the Wellington.

RARE ROAST TOPSIDE WITH WARM JERSEY ROYAL SALAD

··· SERVES 4 ···

The Sunday roast with all the trimmings is a great British tradition but at the wrong time of year it can be soporific. This, however, is a lovely take on the Sunday roast for a summer's day.

1kg well-hung beef topside	2 tsp creamed horseradish	2 bunches watercress, thick stalks removed
salt and pepper	2 tbsp crème fraîche	
200g Jersey royal potatoes	2 tsp olive oil	sea salt and coarsely ground pepper, to serve
sprig of mint		

1 Heat the oven to 220°C/Gas 7. Season the beef liberally. Place on a roasting tray and blast in the oven for 20–30 minutes, until the beef looks well browned. Turn the heat down to 160°C/Gas 3 and cook for a further 30 minutes or until – if you have a meat probe – the internal temperature is 55°C. Remove from the oven and rest for 20 minutes before carving.

2 To make the salad, boil the Jersey royals in salted water with the mint for about 25 minutes. Mix the creamed horseradish, crème fraîche and oil in a large bowl. Drain the potatoes and, while still warm, toss in the horseradish cream. Add the watercress, toss and season with plenty of sea salt and coarsely ground pepper. The warmth of the potatoes will slightly wilt the watercress. Serve on a big plate. Slice the beef thinly and scatter on top.

BEST-EVER GLAZED CARROTS

··· SERVES 4 ···

Baby carrots or ones that come in a bunch are best for these.
Peel or just scrub thoroughly.

8 smallish carrots, topped	1 tbsp butter	small bunch of parsley, leaves picked and chopped
pinch of salt	sprig of thyme	
1 tbsp caster sugar		freshly cracked black pepper

1 Put the carrots in a layer in a wide saucepan and just cover with water. Bring to the boil. Add the salt, sugar, butter and thyme. Put the lid on and gently simmer for 10 minutes, after which the carrots should be cooked through and most of the liquid will have evaporated, leaving behind a beautiful saucy glaze.

2 Reduce with the lid off if there is a little too much. You want the carrots to be lightly coated. Finish with parsley and black pepper.

VENISON HAUNCH WITH SWEET AND SOUR ONIONS

··· SERVES 4 ···

Henry: Venison haunch is from the leg of a deer. It is best cut into thick steaks, fried quickly in plenty of butter, rested and sliced thinly. It has more flavour than fillet or loin, and if cooked properly is beautifully tender. The sweet and sour onions cut the gamey-ness of the venison perfectly. Sweetcorn with garlic mash (see page 208) makes the perfect accompaniment to this dish.

4 venison haunch steaks	knob of butter	splash of rapeseed oil
salt and pepper	**FOR THE SWEET AND SOUR ONIONS:**	4 tbsp white wine vinegar
splash of rapeseed oil	2 onions, thinly sliced	2 tbsp medlar or redcurrant jelly
sprig of rosemary	sprig of thyme	

1 First make the sweet and sour onions. Gently sweat the onions and thyme in a little oil for 5 minutes until soft but not coloured. Pour in the vinegar and jelly and cook for 5 minutes until syrupy and glossy. Season and set aside.

2 Season the venison well. Heat a large frying pan and add the oil. Brown the steaks on each side for 3 minutes – you want a nice brown crust. Turn the heat down a little and add the rosemary and butter. Cook the venison to your liking, depending on how thick they are (see page 168).

3 Remove and rest for 5 minutes before thinly slicing and serving with the sweet and sour onions.

Henry's tip: To make a quick pan sauce, in the frying pan after the venison is finished, pour a small glass of red wine and boil until almost gone. Stir in a large pinch of flour, a teaspoon of medlar jelly and a splash of vinegar. Add a small glass of stock and season. Boil until you have a nice sauce that has a little body to it.

CHICKEN AND LEEK PIE
··· SERVES 6 ···

Tom: I created this for the heads of the National Association of Master Bakers, and in the pie-off I won over Henry's Apple Pie on page 228. (Henry thought it was rigged.) I didn't want to do anything fancy, just make a classic pie and get all the elements right. Served up on a cold winter's day, this ticked all the boxes. These people judge baking competitions, and they like things to measure up to the standards that have been set. So if you want to play it safe with a classic pie, this is it. It doesn't try to do anything else. The thyme and the wine, the tarragon and the crème fraîche make this a timeless classic. This is a pie for people who like things done by the book.

good knob of butter	2 heaped tbsp plain flour	**FOR THE SHORTCRUST PASTRY:**
3 leeks, washed and shredded	125ml good white wine	600g strong white flour
salt and pepper	250ml crème fraîche	150g cold beef dripping, broken into pieces
small bunch of thyme	small bunch of tarragon, leaves picked and roughly chopped	150g cold butter, diced
6 boneless, skinless chicken thighs, diced	egg wash: 1 egg beaten with a pinch of salt	2 tbsp ice-cold water
6 rashers bacon, chopped		

1 Heat the oven to 200°C/Gas 6. To make the pastry, put the flour in a bowl and rub in the lard and butter until the mixture resembles breadcrumbs. Add enough of the cold water to bring the dough together. Wrap in cling film and chill for 20 minutes.

2 Melt the butter in a large frying pan on a medium heat. Add the leeks, salt and pepper and thyme and cook for 10–15 minutes until soft and sweet.

3 Season the chicken. In a separate pan on a high heat, fry the bacon until crispy, then add the chicken and brown off too.

4 Once the leeks are soft, stir in the flour, then add the wine and cook for a couple of minutes until the alcohol has cooked off. Stir in the browned chicken and bacon, then the crème fraîche and tarragon. Set aside to cool.

5 Cut the pastry in half and roll each piece out to about the thickness of a pound coin. Use one sheet to line the bottom of a pie dish. Fill it with the cooled chicken and leek mixture, then lay the other sheet on top.

6 Use your fingers to crimp and pinch around the outside to seal the pie. If you like, make a design for the top with the offcuts. Brush with egg wash and bake for 25 minutes until golden brown.

GRILLED YOUNG LEEKS WITH CHOPPED EGG DRESSING

··· SERVES 4–6 ···

When spring is in the air, this side will help dust away the cobwebs of winter. Light green, tender leeks with little char marks make for a beautiful sight, and the egg dressing works a treat.

8–12 baby leeks	1 tbsp fine capers
1 tbsp extra virgin olive oil	pinch of chopped tarragon
FOR THE EGG DRESSING:	1 egg, boiled for 8 minutes, cooled and peeled
2 tbsp crème fraîche	
1 tsp white wine vinegar	salt and pepper

1 In a small bowl, mix the crème fraîche, vinegar, capers and tarragon. Roughly chop the egg and mix through. Try not to break up the egg too much. Season.

2 Bring a pan of salted water to the boil, add the leeks and cook for 3 minutes. Meanwhile, heat up a griddle pan to smoking hot.

3 Drain the leeks and allow to steam for 2 minutes, then drizzle with olive oil and place on the grill. Char for a few minutes all over. When nice and crispy, put on a serving dish and dress with chopped egg dressing.

ROASTED PUMPKIN WITH SEEDS

··· SERVES 4 ···

Deeply satisfying, gorgeous looking and probably good for you. Iron Bark pumpkins have a beautiful orange colour and flavour. Squashes would work as a substitute.

1 small Iron Bark pumpkin	1 tsp smoked paprika	30g pumpkin seeds
2 tbsp olive oil	2 sprigs of rosemary, leaves picked and chopped	
1 garlic clove, chopped		
2 tbsp maple syrup	salt and pepper	

1 Heat the oven to 180°C/Gas 4. Cut the pumpkin into wedges about 5cm thick and put in a roasting tin. Mix all the remaining ingredients (except the seeds) in a small bowl. Using your hands, smother the pumpkin all over, then roast in the oven for 30 minutes.

2 After 30 minutes scatter the seeds over the top and cook for a further 10 minutes. The pumpkin should be tender and glazed all over.

ASPARAGUS WITH GREEN SAUCE
··· SERVES 4 ···

Henry: This is one of my favourite vegetable sides. Asparagus is best home-grown in late spring and summer. As for the green sauce, these are five ingredients that make the most wonderful of dressings, which will keep in a jar in the fridge for several days.

big bunch of asparagus	2 tbsp fine capers	100ml extra virgin olive oil or rapeseed oil
FOR THE GREEN SAUCE:	3 anchovy fillets (tinned ones)	
2 garlic cloves	1 large bunch of flat-leaf parsley	

1 For the sauce, crush the garlic, chop the capers, dice the anchovies, tame the parsley (pick off all the leaves and chop them), mix together with the oil and leave for 1 hour to infuse. Voilà! Green sauce. Ready for action.

2 To remove the tough lower stalk of the asparagus, carefully bend it until it snaps. It will snap at the woodiest part, where it's most brittle. Use the broken-off pieces for soups.

3 Bring a pan of salted water to the boil and blanch the asparagus for 2–3 minutes. Drain and dress with green sauce.

PUDDING

HENRY

Pudding for me means a proper job. Nothing namby-pamby or fancy. Something rich, comforting, soothing and traditional. 'Dessert' it is not!

TOM

You could go through life without pudding, but it wouldn't be so much fun. It's an indulgence. It's where you seal the deal if you're entertaining, or wooing.

JULIET'S FOOL

JELLY AND ICE CREAM WITH SHORTBREAD

RHUBARB KNICKERBOCKER GLORY WITH PISTACHIOS

APPLE PIE

TOFFEE-APPLE YORKIES

STICKY TOFFEE PUDDING

SALTED CARAMEL TART

RICH CHOCOLATE ORANGE MOUSSE

TREACLE TART

JULIET'S FOOL

··· SERVES 8 ···

A deliciously naughty pud, inspired by the comic characters of Shakespeare as much as his romantic heroine, and made with rich Midlands chocolate, tart raspberries and thick cream.

FOR THE SPICED BISCUITS:

125g unsalted butter, softened

60g golden caster sugar

1 egg yolk

a good pinch each of ground ginger, cinnamon, black pepper, white pepper

1 tsp vanilla extract

150g plain white flour

60g golden caster sugar mixed with a pinch of ground ginger, cinnamon and white pepper

FOR THE RASPBERRY SAUCE:

200g raspberries

2 tbsp icing sugar

juice of half a lemon

FOR THE CHOCOLATE SAUCE:

200g good quality dark chocolate (we used Cadbury's Bournville)

50ml double cream

50ml whole milk

FOR THE CHANTILLY CREAM:

400ml double cream

a little chopped fresh mint

3 tbsp icing sugar

1 vanilla pod, split open

TO SERVE:

fresh raspberries

chopped hazelnuts

sprigs of mint

1 For the biscuits, beat the butter and caster sugar in a bowl until light and fluffy: 2–3 minutes with an electric beater, longer by hand. Mix in the egg yolk, spices and vanilla. Sift the flour over, and mix in well. Shape into a log 8–10cm long, wrap in cling film and firm up in the fridge for 20 minutes.

2 Heat the oven to 180°C/Gas 6. Line a baking tray with baking paper. On a clean surface, sprinkle the spiced sugar, and roll the chilled biscuit log in it. Slice off 1cm-thick ovals with a sharp knife and place on the lined tray. You should get about 16. Bake for 8 minutes until pale gold, and then transfer to a cooling rack.

3 Blend the ingredients for the raspberry sauce until smooth. Put through a sieve to get rid of pips.

4 Put all the ingredients for the chocolate sauce into a thick-bottomed saucepan over a gentle heat and stir until the chocolate has melted.

5 For the Chantilly cream, combine the double cream, mint and icing sugar in a bowl. Extract the vanilla seeds from the pod with the tip of a knife and stir into the cream. Whisk to soft peaks. Add some of the raspberry and chocolate sauces and gently fold through so it's nicely rippled.

6 To assemble, layer whole fresh raspberries, the chocolate sauce, hazelnuts, the rippled cream and the raspberry sauce. Keep layering and then finish with nuts and a sprig of mint, and serve with the spiced biscuits.

JELLY AND ICE CREAM
WITH SHORTBREAD
··· SERVES 6 ···

A jelly made with elderflower, sparkling wine and strawberries, to
be served with home-made shortbread and your favourite ice cream.
A real English summer special.

300ml water	150g strawberries, chopped	pinch of salt
30g caster sugar	**FOR THE SHORTBREAD:**	130g plain flour
500ml English sparkling wine	115g unsalted butter, softened	40g cornflour
4 gelatine leaves	55g golden caster sugar, plus extra for sprinkling	**TO SERVE:**
20ml elderflower pressé		6 scoops of vanilla or mint ice cream

1 First make the shortbread. Heat the oven to 150°C/Gas 2. Line a baking tray with baking paper. Beat the butter and sugar until light and fluffy. This may take a few minutes. Sift the salt, flour and cornflour over the top and gently mix together. Don't overwork the dough. Place the dough on the baking tray and press it out into a square about 5mm thick. Bake for about 30–40 minutes until the shortbread is baked but not browned. Remove and, while still warm, cut into diamond shapes (or shapes of your choice) with a knife. Sprinkle with sugar and cool on a wire rack.

2 Put the water and sugar in a pan, bring to the boil, letting the sugar melt, then bubble for 5 minutes. Set aside.

3 Pour the sparkling wine into a bowl and add the gelatine. After 4 minutes, when the gelatine has softened, pluck it out and add to the sugar syrup. Whisk briskly until dissolved. Pour the gelatine and syrup into the wine bowl, along with the elderflower pressé, stir well and leave to cool for 30 minutes, then put in the fridge for 1 hour or until the mixture starts to thicken. Stir in the strawberries, divide the jelly between 6 serving glasses and refrigerate again for 4 hours or until set.

4 Serve with shortbread biscuits and a scoop of ice cream on top of the jelly.

RHUBARB KNICKERBOCKER GLORY WITH PISTACHIOS

··· MAKES 6 ···

What could be more regency Britain than a knickerbocker glory? A wonderful towering pudding of joy, with layers of rhubarb compote, ice cream, rhubarb jelly, whipped cream, pistachios and wafers. This glory makes the most of forced Yorkshire rhubarb and brings a little sunshine to a bleak winter. It may be a bit of a faff to make, but if you're going to do an extravagant recipe, you might as well do it properly.

FOR THE RHUBARB COMPOTE:

200g forced Yorkshire rhubarb

1 sprig of rosemary

2cm fresh root ginger, chopped

100ml water

75g caster sugar

1 vanilla pod, split and seeds scraped out

FOR THE RHUBARB JELLY:

150ml reserved rhubarb juice, topped up with orange or apple juice if necessary

1 gelatine leaf

FOR THE WHIPPED CREAM:

200ml double cream

30g icing sugar

TO FINISH:

6 scoops of vanilla or ginger ice cream

handful of pistachio nuts, chopped

6 wafers or shortbreads (page 225)

1 Heat the oven to 150°C/Gas 3. Cut the rhubarb into 2.5cm lengths and put into an ovenproof dish. Add the remaining compote ingredients and swish them around. Cover with tin foil and pop into the oven for 25 minutes. Have a check to see if the rhubarb is tender. If not, cook for a bit longer. When done, remove from the oven and leave to cool fully in the dish without stirring (or the rhubarb will go mushy). When cooled, remove the rhubarb to a separate dish, leaving the pink juice.

2 For the rhubarb jelly, sieve the pink rhubarb juice into a small pan. If there is not quite 150ml, top it up with orange or apple juice. Heat it gently up to around 70°C.

3 Meanwhile, soak the leaf gelatine for 4 minutes in a bowl of cold water, then take it out and put it in the warm juice. Stir until melted. Divide between 6 tall glasses and place in the fridge for a few hours to set.

4 Whisk the cream and icing sugar together until thick and firm.

5 To assemble – the fun bit. When the jelly has set, start by putting half a scoop of ice cream in each glass. Spoon in a bit of rhubarb, then a dollop of whipped cream. Repeat the ice cream, rhubarb and whipped cream. The KBG will be looking pretty awesome now. Artfully place 1 remaining bit of rhubarb on top and a scattering of chopped pistachios. Pop a biscuit in, step back, admire, then devour!

APPLE PIE

··· SERVES 6 ···

Henry: This lost to Tom's Chicken and Leek Pie (on page 218), when we were at the National Association of Master Bakers. This is a classic apple pie, pimped up with a little bit of cinnamon and a good bit of lemon.

100g butter

1 large cinnamon stick

6 Cox apples, peeled, cored and chopped

6 Bramley apples, peeled, cored and chopped

100g soft brown sugar

zest and juice of 1 lemon

granulated sugar, to sprinkle

FOR THE SWEET PASTRY:

225g plain flour

100g icing sugar

110g cold unsalted butter, cubed

4 egg yolks

pinch of salt

splash of milk

1 vanilla pod, split and seeds scraped out

1 To make the pastry, mix together the flour and icing sugar then rub in the cold butter until you have a breadcrumby texture. Add the egg yolks, salt, milk and vanilla seeds. Mix it until it comes together, then chill in the fridge for 30 minutes before using.

2 Preheat the oven to 190°C/Gas 5. In a large pan on a medium heat melt the butter until it starts to foam. Add the cinnamon stick, apples, sugar and the zest and juice of the lemon. Reduce the heat to low and cook the apples until they have softened a little but still have a good bit of bite, giving them a stir to break some of them up a little. Allow to cool.

3 Cut the pastry in half then roll each half out until it is about the thickness of a pound coin. Use one sheet to line the bottom of a pie dish, fill with your cooled apple mixture and lay the other sheet over the top. Use your fingers to crimp and pinch around the outside to seal the pie. Sprinkle sugar over the top and bake for 30 minutes until golden brown.

TOFFEE-APPLE YORKIES

··· MAKES 6 ···

This is a wonderful sweet take on the Yorkshire pudding, with a gorgeously rich toffee sauce to accompany it. On page 230 is an equally glorious toffee sauce that happens to be vegan (made without any butter or cream).

FOR THE APPLE YORKSHIRE PUDDINGS:

2 eggs

200ml milk

115g plain flour

1 vanilla pod, split and seeds scraped out

the zest of 1 orange

25g butter, plus extra for greasing

4 apples (russets are best), peeled, cored and cut into eighths

2 tbsp caster sugar, plus extra for sprinkling

FOR THE TOFFEE SAUCE:

50g butter

50g light brown muscovado sugar

50g golden caster sugar

100ml double cream

TO SERVE:

6 scoops vanilla ice cream

1 Heat the oven to 230°C/Gas 8. Put the eggs, milk, flour, vanilla seeds and orange zest in a large mixing bowl, and whisk out all the lumps until you're left with a double-cream consistency. Set aside for 15 minutes.

2 Melt the butter in a pan and add the apples, sugar and a splash of water. Cook for 10 minutes until the apples are soft and caramelized. Add a bit more water as they cook if they look like they are starting to catch.

3 To make the toffee sauce, melt the butter and add the sugars. Heat until the mixture bubbles – do not touch it as it will burn you. Lower the heat and add the cream. Beat well until smooth. Set to one side.

4 Grease a 6-hole jumbo muffin tin with butter and then sprinkle a little sugar into each hole. Divide the apples between the holes and pop in the hot oven for 3 minutes. Pour the batter into a jug to make the next step easier. Remove the hot tray from the oven and quickly pour in the batter until each hole is about half full. Put the tray back into the oven and cook for 10 minutes – do not be tempted to peek.

5 Serve hot, with a scoop of ice cream on top and a drizzle of toffee sauce.

STICKY TOFFEE PUDDING

··· SERVES 6 ···

Tom: This is a proper pudding, for a cold day. The recipe is from the Vegetarian Cookery School in Bath which is run by Rachel Demuth, and is where I taught my very first breadmaking courses, over ten years ago. The quantities for the toffee sauce are large, but that's the best part of a sticky toffee pudding. What's more, this is vegan. Vegans often say they can't get good puddings – this will knock them sideways. This recipe appears in Rachel's beautiful *Green Seasons Cookbook*.

200g dates, halved (and stoned if necessary)	115g soft brown sugar	**FOR THE STICKY TOFFEE SAUCE:**
	⅛ tsp ground nutmeg	100g Golden Syrup
250ml soya milk	¼ tsp ground ginger	150g vegan margarine
100ml water	¼ tsp ground cinnamon	200g soft brown sugar
1 tsp bicarbonate of soda	200g white self-raising flour	1 tsp vanilla extract
115g vegan margarine		100ml soya cream

1 Heat the oven to 190°C/Gas 5. Line a 20cm x 20cm shallow cake tin with baking paper.

2 Put the dates, soya milk and water in a saucepan and simmer gently for 5 minutes until the dates are soft. Take off the heat and stir in the bicarbonate of soda, which will froth as you add it. Set aside to cool.

3 Beat together the margarine and sugar in a bowl until pale and creamy. Add the date mixture and stir it in.

4 Mix the spices into the flour. Sieve the flour and fold it into the sponge mixture. Spoon the sponge mixture into the prepared tin and bake for 35 minutes or until cooked and the sponge bounces back when pressed.

5 For the sauce: melt the syrup, margarine, sugar and vanilla in a small saucepan and simmer for 5 minutes without stirring. Leave to cool slightly and then stir in the soya cream.

6 Prick the pudding all over and pour half the hot toffee sauce over the pudding. Serve the pudding with the rest of the sauce on the side.

SALTED CARAMEL TART

··· SERVES 8 ···

Tom: This has been such a huge favourite all across the country that it was only a matter of time before we made it in the bakery. It's been incredibly popular ever since. The salt-and-caramel taste combination might have been faddy at one point – like chocolate and chilli – but it's stood the test of time. Of all the unlikely flavour juxtapositions, this is one that works.

250g granulated sugar

100ml water

150ml double cream

125g salted butter

1 tsp sea salt flakes, plus extra to sprinkle

FOR THE PASTRY:

250g plain flour, plus extra for dusting

60g sugar

160g salted butter, cubed

1 egg yolk

1–2 tbsp water

TO FINISH:

100g dark chocolate (min. 65% cocoa solids)

30g salted butter

1 You need a 24cm tart tin with a removable base for this. To make the pastry, combine the flour and sugar in a bowl, then rub in the butter until the mixture resembles breadcrumbs. Mix the egg yolk with 1 tablespoon of water, add to the dry ingredients and mix well. You might need a little more water. When the dough comes together, roll it out on a floured work surface – this is a pastry you don't need to rest before rolling – until large enough to fill the tart tin. Drape the pastry over the rolling pin, then drop into the tart tin, gently pressing it into the base. You might need to patch it up in places. Trim the edges. Chill the pastry case in the fridge for at least 20 minutes.

2 Heat the oven to 200°C/Gas 6. Line the pastry case with baking beans and bake 'blind' for 10 minutes. Remove the paper and beans and bake for a further 5–8 minutes to crisp up.

3 Put the sugar and water in a large heavy-based saucepan, bring to the boil slowly over a low to medium heat, then keep bubbling gently until the syrup caramelizes to a dark amber colour. Don't stir: you don't want it to crystallize. If the syrup doesn't reach this amber stage, it won't set as well or have a really glossy finish. Equally, you have to be careful not to go beyond this stage or the syrup will burn. Off the heat, slowly pour in the cream, being careful not to pour too quickly as it will bubble up. If it does, whisk to cool it down. Stir in the butter until melted, add the salt, and pour immediately into the tart case. Set aside to cool.

4 To finish, melt the chocolate and butter in a heatproof bowl over a pan of simmering water until smooth, then drizzle or pipe over the top of the tart. While cooling, sprinkle with a few salt crystals, then leave until cold.

RICH CHOCOLATE ORANGE MOUSSE

··· SERVES 4 ···

Look no further than this stunner for a rich, dark, smooth pudding full
of oohs and aahs. It's easy to knock up in a flash, and it will wow your
diners or sort you out in a moment of fragility. It might use a few bowls
in the making, but it really is worth it. To serve, shortbread biscuits
would be perfect (see page 225) and maybe a few raspberries.

125g chocolate (min. 65% cocoa solids)	75ml milk	3 egg yolks
	zest of 2 oranges	
300ml double cream	125g sugar	

1 Melt the chocolate in a heatproof bowl over a pan of gently simmering water. This should take about 5 minutes. Set to one side.

2 In a second bowl, whisk the double cream until it is semi-whipped and forms soft peaks. A round-bottomed bowl is infinitely easier to whisk in and will be gentler on your arms.

3 Put the milk in a small pan with the orange zest and bring to the boil, then remove from the heat. Set to one side for the orange to infuse the milk.

4 In a third bowl, beat the sugar with the egg yolks. This is to make a kind of sabayon. It is easier with an electric whisk or in a mixer. It will take around 5 minutes and the eggs will be thick and pale yellow in colour when done. It would take a lot longer to do it by hand, but you'd be justified in feeling very proud afterwards.

5 Right, now for crucial fun bit. Pour the orange milk into the sabayon while still mixing. Then scrape the chocolate in and keep whisking. I love it as the white and dark swirl together into one colour. Now, using a large metal spoon, carefully add the whipped cream. Fold it through the chocolate, trying not to knock out too much air. When all is mixed, either spoon into individual pots or into a flattish dish. Place in the fridge to set for 2 hours. Lick the bowl out and contemplate washing up.

TREACLE TART
··· SERVES 6 ···

Tom: This is one of our favourite puddings. It's for when a yogurt or a banana just isn't enough. It warms you up from the inside, while the lemon zest gives it, and you, a little lift. Serve hot with clotted cream or vanilla ice cream. After a pudding like this, you can't do anything other than love the people you're with and enjoy a fire or a brisk walk in the sleet or a howling gale. It's the kind of thing to eat when all the work's been done and you've got nothing left to do but relax. That's when a treacle tart comes into its own: those rare moments when you can actually stop.

450g Golden Syrup	1 small spelt loaf (400g)	160g unsalted butter, cubed
15g butter	**FOR THE PASTRY:**	1 egg yolk
1 egg	250g plain flour, plus extra for dusting	1–2 tbsp water
zest of 1 lemon		
60ml double cream	60g sugar	

1 You need a 24cm tart tin with a removable base for this. To make the pastry, combine the flour and sugar in a bowl, then rub in the butter until the mixture resembles breadcrumbs. Mix the egg yolk with 1 tablespoon of water, add to the dry ingredients and mix well. You might need a little more water. When the dough comes together, roll it out on a floured work surface – this is a pastry you don't need to rest before rolling – until large enough to fill the tart tin. Drape the pastry over the pin, then drop into the tart tin, gently pressing it into the base. Trim the edges. Chill in the fridge for 20 minutes.

2 Heat the oven to 200°C/Gas 6. Line the pastry case with baking beans and bake 'blind' for 10 minutes. Remove the paper and beans and bake for a further 5 minutes to crisp up. Turn the oven down to 180°C/Gas 4.

3 Melt the syrup and butter in a small pan. In a bowl, beat the egg, lemon zest and cream together. When the butter has melted into the syrup, pour it bit by bit into the egg mix.

4 Blitz the bread in a food processor to make breadcrumbs, then add 4 to 5 handfuls (about 120g) into the syrupy mix. (Put the rest of the breadcrumbs in the freezer; they are useful for so many dishes.) Pour the mixture into the pastry case and bake for 15 minutes or until golden and slightly puffed up. Leave to cool for 10 minutes before removing from the tin.

AROUND
MIDNIGHT

HENRY

It's the end of a dinner party, around the dying embers of a fire or a diminishing cheese board, and the conversation has turned to the deep soul of important matters. You don't need a lot of food, you just need a small amount of something sweet, or spicy and intense, or strong and punchy, then a whisky and it's bedtime.

TOM

If the people you are with are just too good to let go, these kinds of snacks will keep the party alive. Or if you've come home late after a long hard day and need something briefly restorative before retiring, you'll find something here.

FIERY FISH BALLS

ANCHOVY SOLDIERS

STINKING BISHOP RAREBIT WITH PLUM CHUTNEY

OATCAKE TRIANGLES AND CHEESE

RHUBARB CHUTNEY

POPPING CANDY TRUFFLES

MINT TRUFFLES

FIERY FISH BALLS

··· MAKES ABOUT 20 ···

Tiny Morecambe Bay shrimps are a famous local delicacy. We've ramped them up here into a seriously grown-up doughnut to fuel the high-octane revellers of Blackpool. These little balls and mind-blowingly good.

FOR THE DOUGHNUTS:	FOR THE FILLING:	FOR THE DUSTING MIX:
100ml milk	2 garlic cloves	1 tbsp salt
large pinch of dried yeast	4 anchovy fillets	1 tbsp caster sugar
250g strong white flour, plus extra for dusting	pinch of sea salt	1 tsp paprika
40g unsalted butter, in cubes	juice and zest of half a lemon	a pinch of cayenne
1 egg yolk	1 free-range egg yolk	
40g caster sugar	50ml olive oil	
a good pinch of sea salt	150g brown shrimps	
vegetable oil, for deep-frying	pinch of freshly chopped parsley	
	salt and pepper	

1 Heat the milk in a small pan until lukewarm. Add the yeast and stir to dissolve it. Set aside. Sieve the flour into a large bowl. Rub in the butter, then add the egg yolk and sugar. Slowly add the milk, then the salt. Bring together into a dough, turn out on a floured surface and knead by hand for at least 10 minutes until it is elastic and smooth (or use a dough hook). Cover the bowl and keep in a warm place for about 45 minutes or until doubled in size.

2 For the filling, mash the garlic and anchovies with the salt and the lemon juice using a pestle and mortar.

3 Put the egg yolk in a bowl, whisk it, then slowly add the oil while continuing to whisk until you have a thick mayonnaise-style sauce. Add the anchovy mixture, then stir in the brown shrimps. Finish with chopped parsley, lemon zest and seasoning.

4 To make each fish ball, take a small amount of dough, about 20g, flatten it in the palm of your hand and place a small amount of the filling in the middle. Close the dough tightly around the filling and roll up the ball between your palms.

5 Combine the ingredients for the dusting mix.

6 Heat the vegetable oil for deep-frying. When hot, use a slotted spoon to put the doughnuts in the hot oil. Fry for 2–3 minutes on one side, then flip over and cook on the other side for about a minute until golden all over. Remove from the oil and drain on kitchen paper. Roll in the dusting mix immediately so it sticks, and then cool slightly before eating.

ANCHOVY SOLDIERS
··· SERVES 1–2 ···

This salty treat is lazy, flavoursome, and great with a Scotch.
For best results, use a close-crumb white bread, such as
a Sherston overnight dough, not a holey sourdough.

2 slices of good white bread	1 tsp finely chopped old-school curly parsley (optional)	
butter		
Gentlemen's Relish or anchovy paste	squeeze of lemon (optional)	
	pepper	

1 Remove the crusts and neaten the edges of the 2 slices of bread, then toast them. Butter one side of one piece. Spread relish on one side of the other piece. Sprinkle the parsley and some drops of lemon juice, if using, over the relish, then twist a little black pepper over it.

2 Press the second slice, buttered-side down, on top. With the palm of your hand, flatten the toast firmly. Cut into skinny soldiers and eat at once.

STINKING BISHOP RAREBIT WITH PLUM CHUTNEY

··· SERVES 4 ···

Stinking Bishop is a soft Gloucestershire cheese, its rind washed in perry.
It's a proper, good, smelly cheese, and we absolutely love it. This might
well be the best rarebit you ever have.

FOR THE RAREBIT:

50g butter

50g plain flour

300ml local beer,
at room temperature

200g Stinking Bishop cheese,
cut into rough pieces

1 tsp Tewkesbury
(or English) mustard

2 tsp Worcestershire sauce

small handful of flat-leaf
parsley, chopped

salt and pepper

4 large slices of bread, preferably
traditional slow-risen bread

olive oil, to drizzle

FOR THE CHUTNEY:

8 plums, stoned and
roughly chopped

3cm fresh root ginger,
grated (about 1 tbsp)

125g soft light brown sugar,
such as muscovado

75ml cider vinegar

1 To make the chutney, heat the plums, ginger, brown sugar and vinegar in a pan over a low heat for approximately 8–10 minutes, or until thick and jammy.

2 For the rarebit, melt the butter in a saucepan and add the flour to make a thick roux. Cook for a couple of minutes, stirring to prevent the roux from catching. Stir in the beer, adding it gradually until you have a thick but smooth sauce. Add the cheese and stir until melted. You should now have a thick paste. Mix in the mustard and Worcestershire sauce, chopped parsley and season to taste.

3 To assemble, drizzle the bread slices with a touch of oil and lightly griddle on each side until nicely char-grilled. Divide the cheesy mix between each slice. Fire the top with a blowtorch for a few minutes (or stick under a preheated hot grill), until browned and bubbling. Serve with the plum chutney.

OATCAKE TRIANGLES

··· MAKES ABOUT 35 OATCAKES ···

This book was oat-fuelled at the start, and so it is at the end. (And see the flapjacks on page 131 in the middle too.) The British – especially the Scots, with the Welsh close behind them – have always loved this highly nutritious and healthy cereal. In other parts of Europe people are less impressed, but we know our oats, and we love them. Oats at night-time are every bit as good as oats for brekkie.

FOR THE OATCAKES:

360g plain flour, plus extra for dusting

2 tbsp caster sugar

½ tsp baking powder

1 tsp sea salt

125g rolled oats, plus extra for sprinkling

100g unsalted butter, cubed

150ml milk

smoked sea salt flakes

TO SERVE:

Wensleydale, or cheese of your choice

rhubarb chutney (see facing page)

1 Heat the oven to 200°C/Gas 6. Put the flour, sugar, baking powder, salt and oats in a large bowl and rub in the butter until you have a breadcrumby texture. Add the milk bit by bit, giving it a good mix until it comes together into a soft dough.

2 Liberally flour a worktop and roll out the dough about 2mm thick. Using a sharp knife, cut the dough into long 5cm-wide strips and then into triangles.

3 Put a large frying pan over a medium-high heat. After about 3 minutes the pan should be hot enough to use. Dry-fry about 8 triangles at a time for 2 minutes or until dark and golden and slightly puffed. Flip over and cook for another 2–3 minutes on the other side.

4 Remove the triangles from the pan with a spatula and place on a cooling rack. Sprinkle with smoked sea salt flakes and leave to cool completely. Serve the biscuits with chutney and cheese.

RHUBARB CHUTNEY
··· MAKES ABOUT 500G ···

A delicious accompaniment to the oatcake triangles with cheese. This is one of our York recipes, and the oatcake shape is a nod to the famous 'rhubarb triangle' of West Yorkshire, producers of the most exquisite forced rhubarb.

small knob of butter

2 banana shallots, finely diced

3cm fresh root ginger, finely chopped

50ml cider vinegar or white wine vinegar

200g light muscovado sugar

half a red chilli, diced

500g rhubarb, chopped into 1cm pieces

½ tsp sea salt

pepper

1 Melt the butter in a saucepan over a medium heat. Add the shallots and ginger and cook until soft and sweet. Add the vinegar, sugar, chilli, rhubarb, salt, and pepper to taste, and bring to the boil. Keep at a rolling boil for about 5 minutes, then reduce the heat and simmer for 15–20 minutes, until slightly thickened.

2 Pour into a sterilized jar (see page 21) and allow to cool.

POPPING CANDY TRUFFLES

··· MAKES ABOUT 25 ···

Tom: Popping candy causes a disco in kids' mouths, and is now being used more widely as a rather trendy ingredient. I recently took some of the Hobbs House Bakery team to Curry Corner in Cheltenham, an institution that has been going for thirty years. Curry Corner were pleased to see all of Hobbs House family and they gave us wonderful service with, to finish, on the house, popping candy truffles borne on a silver tray. They wouldn't give me the recipe, reasonably enough, so I asked Sasha to create a version for us. Everyone loves a truffle – they are small and not so self-indulgent – and these ones go pop in your mouth! You can get the popping candy online or from a good supermarket.

250ml dark chocolate
(min. 65% cocoa solids)

250ml double cream

3 tbsp Golden Syrup

TO FINISH:

50g dark chocolate
(min. 65% cocoa solids)

75g pot of chocolate-covered
popping candy

1 Melt the dark chocolate, double cream and syrup in a bowl set over a pan of simmering water. Once melted and smooth, set aside to cool down, then put in the fridge to firm up, preferably overnight.

2 Line a tray with greaseproof paper. Use a melon baller to scoop out the chocolate ganache into balls and place them on the tray.

3 To finish, melt the chocolate in a bowl over a pan of simmering water, then have it ready in a piping bag. You could use a spoon to drizzle instead.

4 Drop the popping candy on top of the truffles, distributing evenly. Then either pipe or drizzle the chocolate over the truffles and leave to set.

MINT TRUFFLES

··· MAKES ABOUT 30 ···

Pure luxury: white chocolate, essence of mint and flakes of real gold leaf.
These are good after eight, excellent after ten, and divine around midnight.

375g white chocolate	**TO FINISH:**	
40g butter	200g dark chocolate	
180g double cream	(min. 65% cocoa solids)	
2 tsp peppermint oil	edible gold leaf (optional)	
3 tbsp tequila		

1 Melt the white chocolate, butter and double cream in a bowl set over a pan of simmering water. Once melted and smooth, take off the heat and stir in the peppermint and the tequila. Allow to cool down, then put in the fridge to firm up, preferably overnight.

2 Line a tray with greaseproof paper. Use a melon baller to scoop out the chocolate ganache into balls and place them on the tray.

3 To finish, melt the dark chocolate in a bowl over a pan of simmering water. Drop one ball into the chocolate and, using a fork, scoop it out carefully. Holding it just on top of the chocolate, move it up and down, then scrape the bottom on the edge of the bowl to remove excess chocolate. This helps to stop the chocolate pooling on the greaseproof paper. Continue until you've used everything up.

4 As soon as you get the truffle on the paper, add a bit of the gold leaf, if using, before the chocolate sets.

Tom's tip: Edible gold leaf is real, pure gold in minuscule quantities. You can buy it online, and it's perfect for a super-special occasion. If the occasion doesn't call for it, these truffles will still be divinely delicious without it.

INDEX

249

Tom

I would like to start by thanking my wife Anna for pretty much everything, and my ace children, Milo, Beatrix, Josephine and Prudence. I love you all very much. Geoff and Sue, thank you for your support. Big thank you to my brother George, Anna Felton and Emily Wells for helping to keep the boat afloat, and to everyone at Hobbs House Bakery for support and encouragement.

Henry

To my beautiful wife, Jess, and our little girl, Elmer Margot. It's all for you and nothing without.

Anne, Tony and Sam, best in-laws and landlords. Cheers for being supportive.

The butchers and all at Hobbs House. Your hard work and dedication makes what we do possible. Especially Ant Smith, for talking through endless ideas over a pint.

Together

To Trev and Polly (Mum and Dad), the best parents brothers could ask for. Thanks for your huge love. To all our family, for being just wicked and tasting anything we cook for you.

Jessica Stone, Claire Morgan and Chessie Root, from Independent Talent, thank you for helping everything run so smoothly.

Thank you to our uncles Clive Wells and Sam Wells for their support, and to everyone at Hobbs House Bakery, including Keith Strickland, Jenny Coombe, Claire Maslin, William Ugle and Bafana Ncube.

Many people have been involved in the inspiration, creation and testing of our recipes, and in particular we would like to thank Carla Moulder, Sasha Jenner, Antony Smith and Fiona Jarman – we are gargantuanly grateful. To Dan Cooper for his great recipes and grill wisdom, and Maxwell Colonna and Kate Gover for their inspirational passion and expertise. And to Signe Johansen for testing and tying up loose ends when we most needed it.

Anna Jones, Emily Ezekiel, Abi Fawcett, Chris Taylor, Richard Harris and Janet – your creative enthusiasm and hard work has helped make this book so tasty.

To the team that has helped us create a beautiful book. At Headline, a massive thank you to Sarah Emsley, our publisher, and Veronique Norton for making the book tour such a delight. We are hugely indebted to Mari Roberts, our book editor, who has given shape and coherence to our mad ramblings. Chris Terry for the beautiful photos, thank you, sir, and thank you to Alex Smith and his super team at Smith & Gilmour.

Liz Warner, Walter Iuzzolino, what a pleasure it has been to do this all again. Here's to many more. Big thanks to the best crew out there, including Neil Smith, Guernsey Graffalo, Ian Carre, Ed St Giles, Emma Vulliamy, Tom Hayward, Jamie Knight, Geraint, Chris Youle-Grayling, Mike and Joe Sarah, Charlotte Linzell, Lauren Vanderkar, Fay Thompson, Safiyya Abdulla, Hannah Cork, Eleanor Thompson, Callum Howell, Rob Myler.

Katie Horswell and all at C4 – thanks for giving us another shot at it.

To Neil Cross from SVA and Tomas Miller from Miller Howard Workshop for helping make the goods shed event such a success and for the glorious gigantic Igrill that features in this book.

A big thank you to everyone who has stocked this book and our first one, we really appreciate it. And thank you also to all the food and literary festivals that gave us the stage to share what we love to do.

Finally a massive thank you to everyone who is a Baker Brothers fan. If you've loved the TV shows, enjoyed our first book, been to one of our demos, shared tweets of baking success, been on one of our cookery/baking courses, visited us at Hobbs House (Bakery/Butchery/Bistro/Cookery School), then a massive thank you. You truly make it all worthwhile.

twitter @Tom_Herbert_ & @Henry_Herbert